Jossey-Bass Teacher

Jossey-Bass Teacher provides K–12 teachers with essential knowledge and tools to create a positive and lifelong impact on student learning. Trusted and experienced educational mentors offer practical classroom-tested and theory-based teaching resources for improving teaching practice in a broad range of grade levels and subject areas. From one educator to another, we want to be your first source to make every day your best day in teaching. *Jossey-Bass Teacher* resources serve two types of informational needs—essential knowledge and essential tools.

Essential knowledge resources provide the foundation, strategies, and methods from which teachers may design curriculum and instruction to challenge and excite their students. Connecting theory to practice, essential knowledge books rely on a solid research base and time-tested methods, offering the best ideas and guidance from many of the most experienced and well-respected experts in the field.

Essential tools save teachers time and effort by offering proven, ready-to-use materials for in-class use. Our publications include activities, assessments, exercises, instruments, games, ready reference, and more. They enhance an entire course of study, a weekly lesson, or a daily plan. These essential tools provide insightful, practical, and comprehensive materials on topics that matter most to K–12 teachers.

Hands-On Art Activities for the Elementary Classroom

Seasonal, Holiday, and Design Activities for Grades K–5

Judē Cataldo

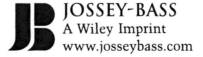

JOSSEY-BASS
A Wiley Imprint
www.josseybass.com

Published by Jossey-Bass
A Wiley Imprint
989 Market Street, San Francisco, CA 94103-1741   www.josseybass.com

Jossey-Bass books and products are available through most bookstores. To contact Jossey-Bass directly call our Customer Care Department within the U.S. at 800-956-7739, outside the U.S. at 317-572-3986, or fax 317-572-4002.

Jossey-Bass also publishes its books in a variety of electronic formats. Some content that appears in print may not be available in electronic books.

Library of Congress Cataloging-in-Publication Data
Cataldo, Judē (date)
Hands-on art activities for the elementary classroom: seasonal, holiday, and design activities for grades K–5 / Judē Cataldo.—1st ed.
p. cm.
ISBN: 978-0-471-56339-6

1. Education, Elementary—Activity programs. 2. Creative activities and seat work. 3. Art—Study and teaching (Elementary) 4. Holidays—Study and teaching (Elementary)—Activity programs—United States. 5. Seasons—Study and teaching (Elementary)—Activity programs—United States. I. Title.
LB1592.C37 2006
372.5'044—dc22
2006010555

FIRST EDITION
PB Printing   10 9 8 7 6 5 4 3 2 1

About This Book

Art teachers are a special breed. Some of you may not have the luxury of teaching in your own classroom, so you cart all of your belongings in large bags from room to room. How can you still be able to meet your students' every creative need, even if you are short on space? This book of eighty seasonal, holiday, and design projects will help you.

The main theme in teaching is adaptability—and as an art teacher you know this better than anyone else. You understand curriculum needs, grade-level needs, holiday needs, and just plain "it's a full moon, let's keep it simple" needs. You are a "Jack (or Jill) of all trades" who needs to know how to evaluate each student's strengths quickly. This book will help you do that—and more—by offering inexpensive tools and materials that will help make your teaching day easier to handle.

The eighty projects are arranged in four sections: *Fall, Winter, Spring/Summer,* and *Design Activities.* Each project follows the same format:

- Activity Title
- Grade Level
- Background
- Project Description
- Advance Preparation
- Materials Needed
- Connections to Other Disciplines
- Teacher Directions
- Student Directions

You'll find drawings that illustrate many of the step-by-step directions for creating the project as well as full-page patterns that are ready to copy and give to students.

Obtaining Materials

Don't be afraid of being called a "junk collector"! Found objects—like twigs, rocks, cardboard, Styrofoam, and magazines—make great materials for projects. There are plenty of free supplies everywhere you look.

Become friends with the cafeteria staff. These wonderful people can supply you with great materials, such as Styrofoam trays, plastic utensils, and empty egg and milk cartons (just be sure to clean and rinse before using). The janitorial staff can also be great friends. They know when boxes and newspapers are ready to be tossed out.

Remember, too, that art supplies "grow wings," so be sure to check all supplies at the end of each class.

Managing Class Time

Allow about ten minutes to introduce the project and distribute materials, and about ten minutes after the project to clean up—on a good day! (Remember to be flexible.)

Rely on your most difficult students to help with setting up the materials so that these students feel important. A little trust and respect go a long way.

Ask those students who have completed their projects to be mentors to other students who may need some help. Remember, you can't be everywhere at any one time!

A Final Word

Art is a process as well as a result. You know your students, so go with what works. Feel free to adapt projects according to the needs and abilities of your students. Everyone can draw *something*. As Pablo Picasso said: "The important thing is to create. Nothing else matters; creation is all."

I hope you and your students will enjoy creating together all year long!

Judē Cataldo

About the Author

Judē Cataldo is an elementary art teacher in Union City, New Jersey, a multicultural community. She has taught art to special education students for the Mount Carmel Guild Schools and elementary, middle, and secondary art in the Union City schools.

In addition to teaching, Judē has been a graphic designer and illustrator for Prentice Hall, Scholastic, and Troll Associates publishers. She has illustrated and designed for educational and business and professional books. She has also designed over one hundred book covers.

Judē graduated from Kean University with a bachelor's of fine arts and a K–12 teaching degree. She continued her illustrating studies for over ten years at Parsons School of Design and School of Visual Arts in New York City. She also received a computer graphics certificate from Bergen Community College and ESL certification from New Jersey City University.

A talented photographer and painter, Judē has exhibited in galleries and libraries and at art festivals and is the recipient of several art awards.

To my beloved mother, Anne, you are my sound and my light.
A special thanks to the one who started a dream,
Winfield Huppuch, Evelyn Fazio, Agnes Dauerman,
the Edison School teachers, Patty Ardente, Mrs. Fazio, Laurie Reed;
and who helped put the dream together, Diane Turso.

Contents

Winter

Spring and Summer

Design Activities

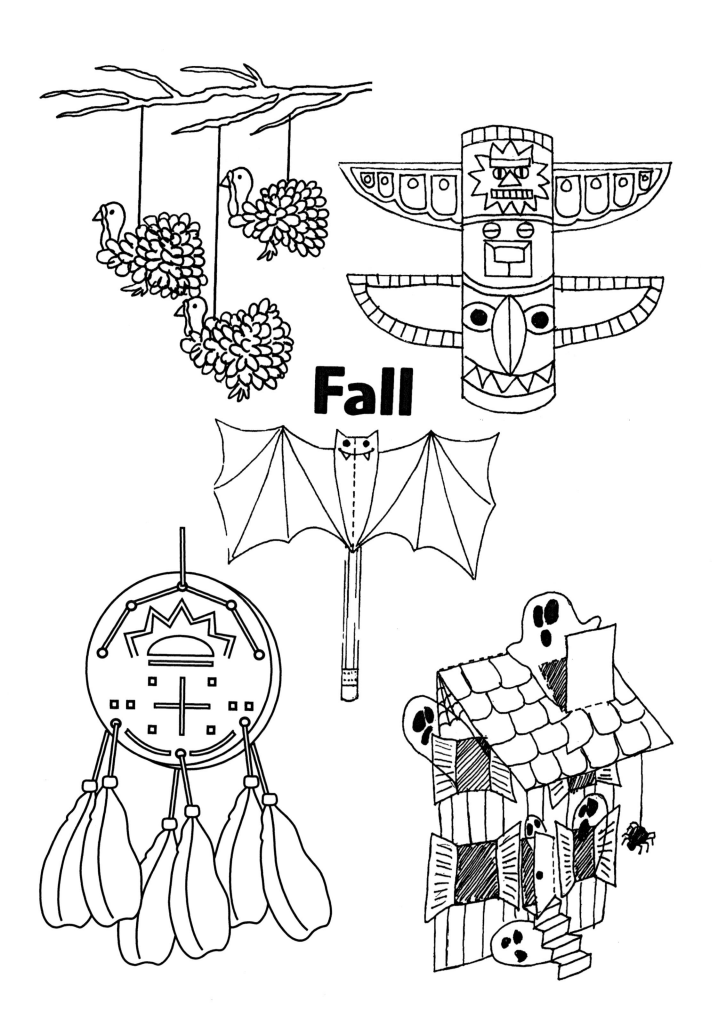

Fall

General

1. SUNFLOWER GARDEN

Grade Level: K–2

Sunflowers are a colorful part of fall in many parts of the country. They are the only single flower that can grow as high as ten feet. The sunflower is native to North America; Native Americans used it for food and pressed the seeds for hair oil. Today, the seeds are used for oil, birdseed, and snacks. The seeds are rich in calcium.

Project Description

Students will create sunflowers using paper plates, construction paper, and birdseed.

Advance Preparation

Obtain enough small paper plates to have one for every student. Buy paper cups and birdseed. Cut green construction paper into one 2" x 18" strip and two leaf shapes for each student. Pour the birdseed into paper cups. Make a finished sunflower to show the students.

Materials Needed

Scissors

Green construction paper

Yellow construction paper

Small paper plates

White glue

Craft stick

Bag of mixed birdseed for outdoor birds (enough for 1/2 cup per student; about one 5-pound bag per class)

Paper cups

Crayons

Tape

Newspaper to cover work area

2

Connections to Other Disciplines

Science: Discuss sunflowers—where they grow, how tall they can get, and what they can be used for (food, hair oil, calcium-rich snacks).

Cooking: Bring in sunflower seeds for the students to snack on.

Reading: Introduce *And a Sunflower Grew* by Aileen Lucia Fisher.

Teacher Directions

1. Cover the work area with newspaper.
2. Give each student a paper plate, a 2" x 18" strip of green construction paper, and two leaf shapes.
3. Distribute the rest of the materials.
4. Show students the sample project.
5. Help students with cutting and pasting.

Student Directions

1. Cut thirty 12" petals from the yellow construction paper, and glue them around the edge of the paper plate.
2. Use a craft stick to spread glue over the center of the paper plate.
3. Sprinkle birdseed over the glue, and gently shake off any excess birdseed. Let dry.
4. Glue a stem and two leaves in place. Use a crayon to add veins to the leaves.
5. Tape the sunflower along with your classmates' sunflowers on a wall in the classroom to create a "garden."

2. OWL'S HOME

Grade Level: 2–3

Owls are often heard in the woods in the fall. Owls are birds that have large eyes and fine depth perception (ability to judge distance). They have the most highly developed sense of hearing of all birds. An owl can fly through a forest in silence because its wing feathers have downy fringes to muffle the sound of its approach. All of these characteristics help the owl catch its prey. Owls make their nests in cavities of trees.

Project Description

Students will create an owl and its tree using paper and crayons.

Advance Preparation

Make copies of the owl pattern sheet, cut apart at the cut lines, and give one owl to each student. Have enough brown construction paper on hand to give a sheet to each student.

Materials Needed

Owl pattern sheets

Sheets of scrap drawing paper

Crayons

8" x 12" sheets of brown construction paper

Black markers

Scissors

Tape

Connections to Other Disciplines

Science: Talk about where owls live. What do they eat? Why are their eyes large?

Language Arts: Discuss the expression "As wise as an owl." Have students make up a story about their owl.

Mathematics: Show how an owl can be drawn using circles, triangles, and patterns.

4

Teacher Directions

1. Give each student one owl pattern sheet and one sheet of brown construction paper.
2. Distribute the rest of the materials.
3. Show students how to make contour lines.
4. Help students cut out the C in the brown paper.

Student Directions

1. Practice drawing contour lines on the scrap paper with crayons.
2. When comfortable making contour lines, use a black marker to draw contour lines on the brown paper so that the paper looks like tree bark.
3. Draw a large C in the center of the brown paper. Cut along the C to form a flap.

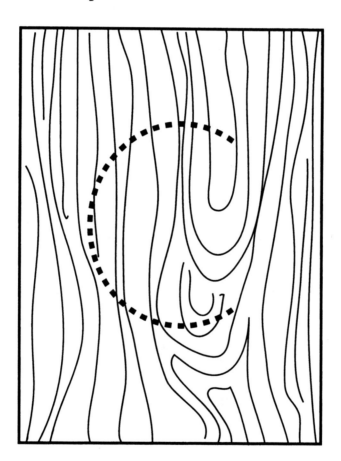

4. Use crayons to color the owl.
5. Place the finished owl behind the cut-out C flap and tape it in place. Fold back the flap so you can see the owl.

3. POINTILLIST AUTUMN LANDSCAPE

Grade Level: 3–4

The painter Georges Seurat (1859–1891) developed the style of painting called *Pointillism*, using small spots of pure color. When viewed from a distance, the light rays reflected from the adjacent colors merged to produce a blended hue of different colors. The effect created a luminous moving color exchange.

Project Description

Students will learn how to use a new watercolor and craypas technique to create a three-dimensional autumn landscape.

Advance Preparation

Find examples of Pointillist paintings, especially some by Georges Seurat, to show to students. Have available several Styrofoam packing "peanuts" and two sheets of white watercolor paper for each student.

Materials Needed

White watercolor paper

Watercolors

Craypas

Scissors

Paintbrushes

Water cups

Packing peanuts

White glue

Newspaper to cover work area

Connections to Other Disciplines

Science: Discuss interaction of colors, the light spectrum, and refraction.

Reading: Introduce *The Lives of Artists* (series) by Kathleen Krull.

Teacher Directions

1. Describe Pointillism. Show examples by famous artists, such as Georges Seurat.
2. Cover the work area with newspaper.
3. Give each student two sheets of watercolor paper.
4. Hand out the rest of the materials.
5. Help students create the background and trees using dots and bright colors.

Student Directions

1. On one sheet of paper, paint a fall foliage scene using watercolors to make dots.
2. On a separate sheet of paper, use craypas to draw tree shapes. Color in the trees with dots.

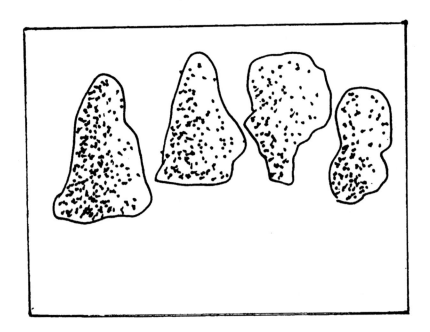

3. Cut out the trees and glue two or three packing peanuts to the back of each tree.

4. Glue the trees to your watercolor background.

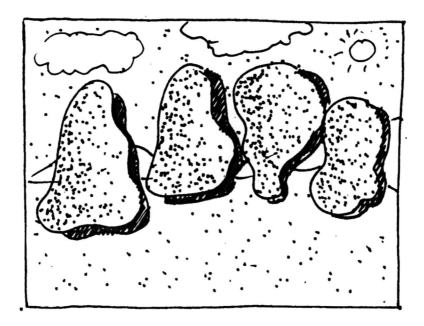

4. HARVEST APPLE

Grade Level: 3–4

John Chapman, known as Johnny Appleseed, is an American legend. It's believed that he helped spread apple trees across the country in the late 1700s and early 1800s.

Project Description

Students will create three-dimensional apples.

Advance Preparation

Cut newspaper into strips or use recycled strip paper. Make two copies of the apple pattern sheet for each student.

Materials Needed

Apple pattern sheets

Crayons or craypas

Scissors

Stapler

Newspaper strips or recycled strip paper

String

Connections to Other Disciplines

Science: Discuss the nutritional value of apples in the diet.

Social Studies: Explore the legend of Johnny Appleseed.

Reading/Mathematics: Introduce *Ten Apples Up on Top* by Dr. Seuss (writing as Theo LeSieg) and *The True Tale of Johnny Appleseed* by Margaret Hodges.

Cooking: How many ways can apples be prepared? Make applesauce with the students, or bring some applesauce cake to class.

Teacher Directions

1. Pass out two copies of the apple pattern sheet to each student.
2. Discuss the different colors of apples.
3. Have students color the apple patterns first with light colors, then overlapping with darker colors. Show students how to use complementary colors to create shading.
4. Help students with the stapling.
5. Hang the finished apples in the classroom.

Student Directions

1. Color one apple pattern following your teacher's directions. Then color the second pattern the same way.
2. Cut out the two apples and place them together, colored sides out.
3. Staple two edges together halfway around.
4. Stuff the apple with strips of newspaper.
5. Finish stapling the apple together.
6. Use string to hang your apple in the classroom.

5. LEAF FRAME

Grade Level: 3–4

Here's an activity that incorporates found objects to make a "natural" craft project out of autumn leaves.

Project Description

Students will create a frame with glued leaves.

Advance Preparation

Collect small leaves (or have students collect them) and flatten them under a book for a day or two. Cut an 8" square of cardboard for each student. Cut sponges into 1" squares. Cut four 2" x 8" and two 2" x 7" strips of cardboard for each student. Obtain spray shellac and sponges; cut the sponges into 1" squares, one for each student. Make a completed leaf frame to show to students.

Materials Needed

Cardboard

Leaves

Glue

Spray shellac (CAUTION: To be used only by an adult)

Paints

Sponges

Newspaper to cover work area

Connections to Other Disciplines

Science: How many different shapes of leaves can be found? Which leaf comes from what tree?

Reading: Introduce *Why Do Leaves Change Color?* by Betsy Maestro.

Teacher Directions

1. Show students your sample of the finished frame.
2. Cover the work area with newspaper.
3. Give each student an 8" square piece of cardboard, four 2" x 8" strips and two 2" x 7" strips of cardboard, and a 1" square piece of sponge.

4. Distribute the rest of the materials.

5. Help students form their frames.

6. Take the finished frames outdoors and spray with the shellac.

Student Directions

1. Make a frame by gluing the four 2" x 8" cardboard strips together in the shape of a frame. Overlap the side strips on top and bottom strips and glue the corners together; the sides of the frame do not have to be flush. The window of the frame will be a 4" x 4" space. Attach the frame to the 8" square cardboard backing and glue the two 2" x 7" strips onto the backing. Let dry.

2. Use the paint and sponges to apply color to your frame. Let dry.

3. Glue pressed leaves to the frame. Let dry.

4. Your teacher will bring your frame outdoors to spray with shellac. When it's dry, you can put an item or picture in your frame.

Columbus Day

6. THE *NIÑA*, THE *PINTA*, AND THE *SANTA MARIA*

Grade Level: 3–4

Christopher Columbus sailed from Spain in 1492 to find a shorter passage to the East Indies, where precious spices and rare cloth could be found. His three ships, the *Niña,* the *Pinta,* and the *Santa Maria,* landed on the island of Hispaniola (now home to Haiti and the Dominican Republic) in the Caribbean. This is considered to be Europeans' first contact with the New World. Columbus Day is observed on the second Monday in October.

Project Description

Students will create a picture of Christopher Columbus's three ships using cut paper. (*Note:* This project is done in three lessons.)

Advance Preparation

Using the pattern, cut stencils for the ships' hulls out of oak tag (one for each student). Obtain sheets of 8-1/2" x 11" sheets of white construction paper, 9" x 12" brown construction paper, and 12" x 18" blue construction paper (at least one for each student). For younger students, prepare the sails.

Materials Needed

Oak tag

Hull pattern sheets

8-1/2" x 11" sheets of white construction paper

Scissors

Red crayons

9" x 12" sheets of brown construction paper

12" x 18" sheets of blue construction paper

White glue

White chalk

Tape

Connections to Other Disciplines

Geography: Discuss the seven continents and where they are located. Find Hispaniola on a map.

Social Studies: Discuss why Christopher Columbus made his trip from Spain.

Reading: Introduce _On the Day the Tall Ships Sailed_ by Betty Paraskevas. (Although this book's level is K–1, other students may still find it interesting.)

Teacher Directions

Lesson 1

1. Hand out the white paper, scissors, and red crayons. For younger students, pass out the sails you have prepared in advance.
2. Help older students fold and cut out the white paper to make sails.

Lesson 2

1. Hand out the brown paper, the ship's hull pattern, scissors, and glue.
2. Help students trace the pattern of the ship's hull on brown paper, then cut out the ship.
3. Help students glue sails onto the masts.

Lesson 3

1. Hand out the blue construction paper, chalk, scissors, and tape.
2. Help students fold and cut the blue paper for the ocean.

Student Directions

Lesson 1

1. Cut the 8-1/2" x 11" white paper in half. You will use one 8-1/2" x 5-1/2" half sheet for your sails.
2. Fold the white paper into eight equal sections.
3. Cut out three sections for the large sails, cut in half three sections for the half sails, and cut two sections in half for the triangle sails. These sections will be the sails for the three boats. There should be four sails for each of the three boats.

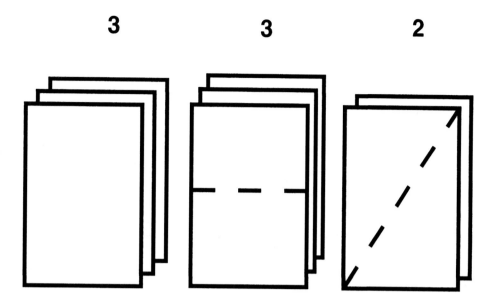

4. Draw a Spanish cross in red on the square and rectangular boxes.

Lesson 2

1. Fold the brown paper into three short sections.
2. Trace the pattern of the boat's hull on the folded paper.
3. Cut out the hull to create three hulls.
4. Cut out nine strips from the brown paper to form masts.
5. Glue three of the brown strips to each hull to make masts.
6. Draw portholes on the ships.
7. Glue the sails to the masts.

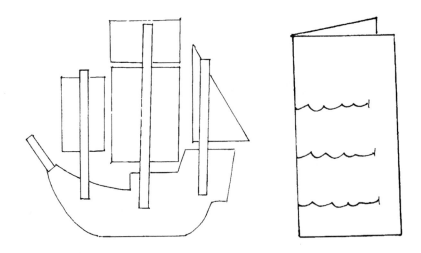

Lesson 3

1. Fold the blue construction paper in half. Using white chalk, draw ocean waves on the paper from the fold line to about 1" from the edge.

2. Cut along the lines of the waves. Open the paper and draw some more waves. Draw some clouds in the sky with the white chalk.

3. Slip the hulls of your completed boats behind the three waves and secure with tape. Put a name on each boat.

4. Write "Columbus Discovers the New World" at the bottom of your picture.

NIÑA

PINTA

SANTA MARIA

COLUMBUS DISCOVERS THE NEW WORLD

18

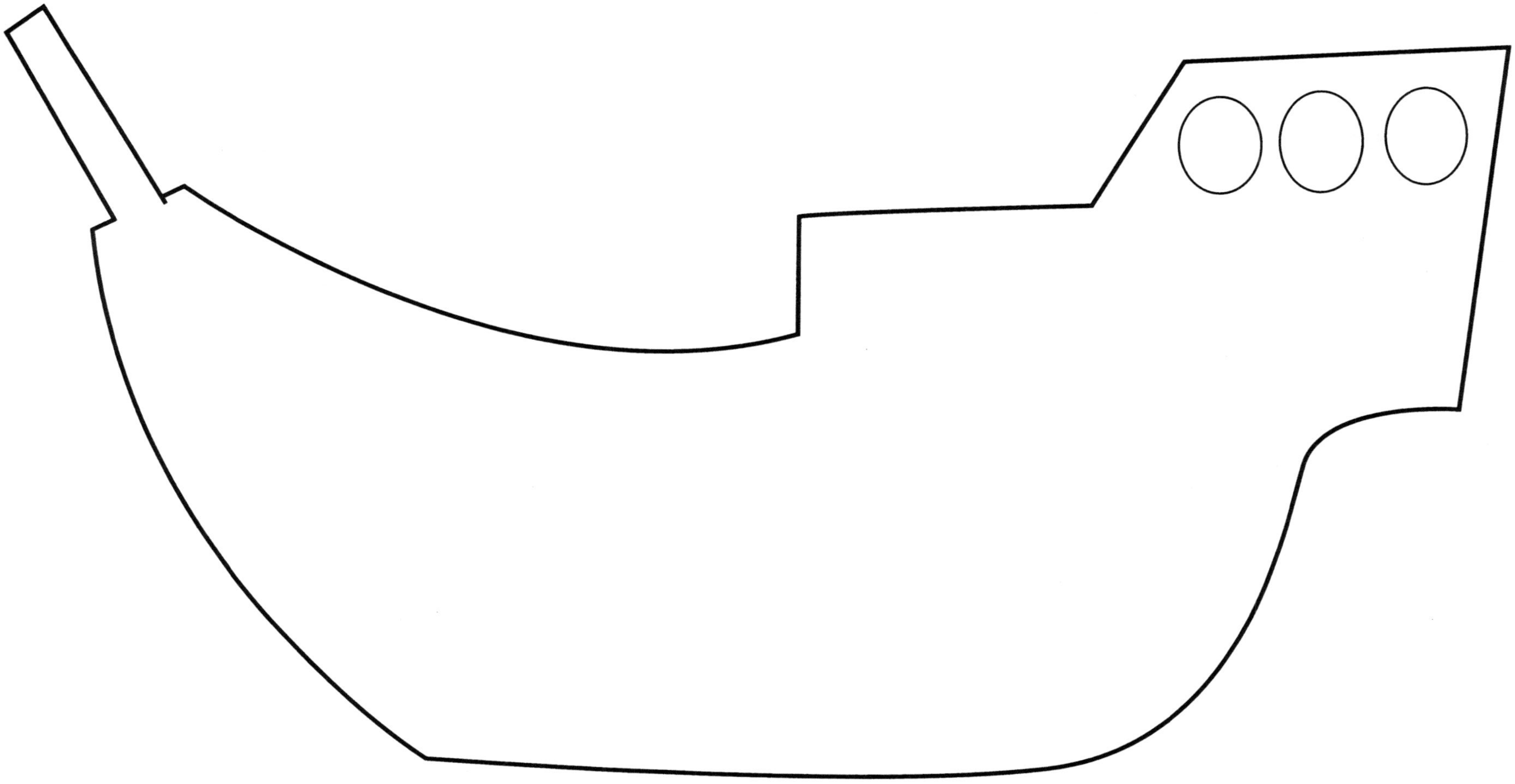

Halloween

7. FLYING BAT

Grade Level: K–2

Why are bats associated with Halloween? Myths about bats come from many sources. The truth is that vampire bats live mostly in South America and are only a small percentage of all bat species. Most bats eat insects or fruits. Bats are important because they help to control the insect population and to reseed forests. They have also given us important information about sonar (the ability to use sound to navigate).

Project Description

Students will create a simple flying bat using black paper and a pencil or straw.

Advance Preparation

Have unsharpened pencils or straws and white chalk for all the students. Have a supply of 9" x 12" black construction paper. Use a pattern sheet to make bat stencils out of oak tag for students to trace. Prepare a model of the finished bat to show the class.

Materials Needed

Oak tag for bat stencil

9" x 12" sheets of black construction paper

White chalk

Scissors

Unsharpened pencils or straws

Tape

Connections to Other Disciplines

Science: Talk about bat behavior. Why are bats important?

20

Teacher Directions

1. Give each student a sheet of 9" x 12" black paper, a bat stencil, and an unsharpened pencil or straw.
2. Distribute the rest of the materials.
3. Show students how to fold the paper in half and trace around the stencil.
4. Show students your model of the bat so they can see where to draw the veins on the wings.
5. Help students cut out their bats and tape them to their pencils.

Student Directions

1. Fold the black paper in half.
2. Use white chalk to trace the bat outline. Be sure the middle of the bat is on the fold line.

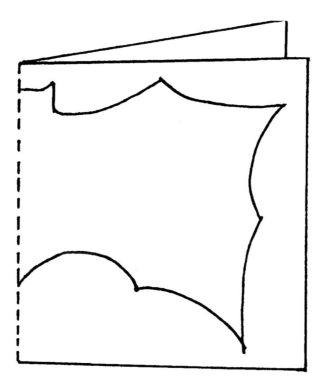

3. Draw the veins on the bat wings.
4. Cut out the bat, but do not cut the fold line. Open the bat.
5. Draw a mouth, eyes, and fangs to make a face.
6. Tape a pencil or straw to the back of the bat on the fold.
7. Slowly move the pencil or straw up and down to make the bat fly!

8. CLOTHESLINE GHOST

Grade Level: 1–2

Here's a fun activity to help get your students in the mood for Halloween!

Project Description

Students will make ghosts that hang from a clothesline.

Advance Preparation

Have one 12" x 18" sheet of white construction paper for each student. Suspend a clothesline across the room for displaying the completed ghosts.

Materials Needed

Clothesline

12" x 18" sheets of white construction paper

Black markers

Scissors

Tape

Connections to Other Disciplines

Reading: Introduce grade-level Halloween joke and riddle books, such as *Creepy Riddles* by Katy Hall and Lisa Eisenberg.

Teacher Directions

1. Draw the ghost on the chalkboard for students to copy.
2. Give each student a sheet of 8" x 18" white construction paper, a black marker, and scissors.

Student Directions

1. Copy the ghost shape that's drawn on the chalkboard.
2. Draw a face on your ghost.

3. Cut out your ghost and fold over the tops of the hands as shown.

4. Hang your ghost by the hands on the clothesline your teacher has strung across the room. You might want to tape the hands in place so that your ghost hangs on!

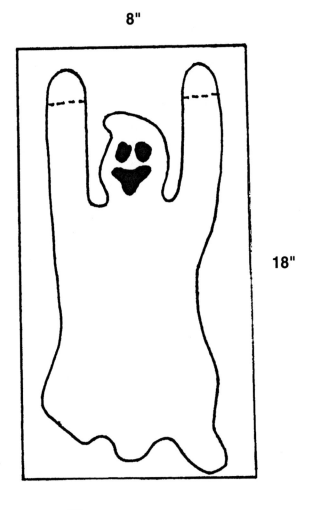

8"

18"

Hands-On Art Activities

9. HAUNTED HOUSE

Grade Level: 1–3

The haunted house may have originated with the Druids and Celts in ancient England and Ireland, who believed that spirits of the dead would come back to Earth in the forms of animals (such as bats, spiders, and black cats) or as human ghosts and spirits. These spirits would remain where they were when their bodies were killed or died unexpectedly, thus creating a house that was haunted.

Project Description

Students will create a three-dimensional haunted house with ghosts. *(Note:* This project is done in three lessons.)

Advance Preparation

Prepare a finished house to show as a model. Have white drawing paper, black construction paper, and a 12" x 18" sheet of gray construction paper for each student. Make a copy of the haunted house pattern sheet for each student.

Materials Needed

Haunted house pattern sheets

12″ x 18″ sheets of gray construction paper

White drawing paper

Black construction paper

Crayons

Scissors

Glue

White string

Connections to Other Disciplines

Social Studies: Discuss the history of Halloween. Who were the ancient Druids and Celts?

Reading: Introduce grade-level books about Halloween, such as *Cranberry Halloween* by Wende and Harry Devlin.

Teacher Directions

Lesson 1

1. Show the class your finished house
2. Give each student a haunted house pattern sheet, a sheet of 12" x 18" gray construction paper, and crayons.
3. Help students draw the door, windows, and chimney box.

Lesson 2

1. Pass out the white paper and scissors.
2. Show students how to cut out the door, windows, chimney, and ghosts.
3. Assist students as needed in decorating the house.

Lesson 3

1. Pass out the black construction paper and glue.
2. Help students glue on the ghosts, make and glue on the stairs, and make and hang the spiders.

Student Directions

Lesson 1

1. Fold over the top quarter portion of the gray construction paper to make a roof.
2. Draw in four windows and a door as shown on the pattern. On the folded flap, draw a box for the chimney.

Lesson 2

1. Draw wooden planks on the front of the house and tiles on the roof. Tiles on the roof can be cut out with additional colored paper for added dimension. Draw a vertical line down the center of each window.
2. Cut out the door, windows, and chimney on three sides so they open out, as shown in the illustration.
3. Cut out ghosts from white paper and draw on their facial features.

Lesson 3

1. Glue ghosts in the door and windows of your house.
2. Make stairs by folding a 3" x 6" piece of paper (the width of the door) in accordion pleats.
3. Glue the stairs to the doorsill so that they hang down.
4. Cut a spider from black construction paper. Use white string to hang the spider from the roof. Your haunted house is complete!

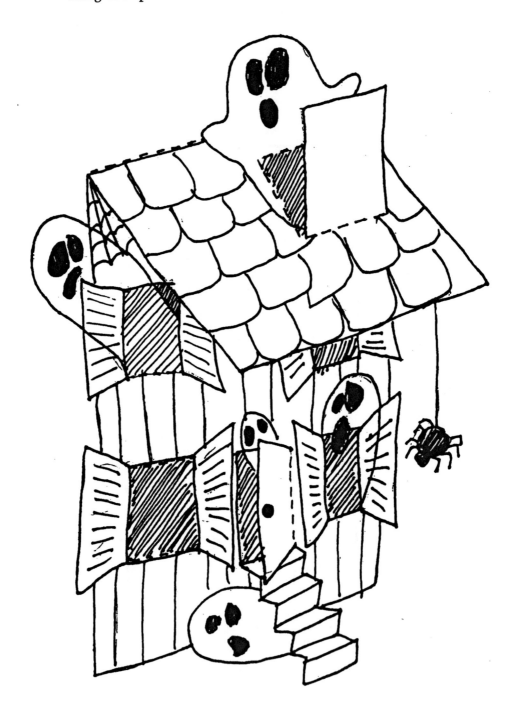

10. PUMPKIN FACE

Grade Level: 2–3

The first jack-o'-lanterns, made in Ireland long ago, were carved from turnips or beets. In England, small lanterns are called "punkies" for small pumpkins. They help to light the way on a dark night!

Project Description

Students will draw pumpkin characters.

Advance Preparation

Copy the pictures from this book or from another book, or create your own pictures of faces on pumpkins to show students as examples. Have one 18" x 24" sheet of white paper for each student.

Materials Needed

18" x 24" sheets of white paper

Crayons or markers

Connections to Other Disciplines

Social Studies: Ask students to explain the connection between carving pumpkins and Halloween.

Reading: Introduce students to *The Pumpkin Smasher* by Anita Benarde and *The Biggest Pumpkin Ever* by Steven Kroll.

Cooking: Give your students tastes of pumpkin pie, pumpkin bread, pumpkin cookies—whatever recipes you can find.

Teacher Directions

1. Show students the examples of jack-o'-lantern faces.
2. Give each student one sheet of 18" x 24" white paper.
3. Pass out the crayons and markers.

Student Directions

1. Draw the outline of a pumpkin on the white paper.
2. Choose a character and draw the facial features on the pumpkin.
3. Color in the pumpkin character.

30

Hands-On Art Activities

Day of the Dead

11. SKULL

Grade Level: 3–5

The Day of the Dead (Dia de los Muertos) is celebrated mainly in Mexico on the first and second days of November. It is believed that the deceased are given divine consent to visit their relatives and friends on Earth. These nonthreatening souls make sure all is well and that they have not been forgotten. The skull folk art created for this occasion is also not meant to be scary.

Project Description

Students will create a design using yarn to outline a skull and fill in the background with concentric designs.

Advance Preparation

Make a finished skull to show the students. Make a copy of the skull pattern sheet for each student. Have available several colors of yarn and cardboard for support.

Materials Needed

Yarn in several bright colors	Scissors
Skull pattern sheets	Cardboard
White glue	Pencils or sticks

Connections to Other Disciplines

Mathematics: Discuss and illustrate concentric lines. (Concentric lines have a common center. A pattern is created by enlarging or decreasing the distance from the center.)

Science: Think of shapes found in nature that are textural and concentric, such as pond ripples, tree bark, veins of leaves, sliced onions, and crop rows on a farm.

Social Studies: Ask students: How is death viewed by different cultures?

Reading: Although the following two books' level is K–1, other students may still find them interesting. Introduce *Day of the Dead* by Tony Johnston and *Festival of the Bones: El Festival de las Calaveras* by Luis San Vicente. A book for second and third grades is *Pablo Remembers: The Fiesta of the Day of the Dead* by George Ancona.

Teacher Directions

1. Discuss the Day of the Dead and the use of the skull symbol in Mexican folk art. Show students the finished sample.
2. Give each student one skull pattern sheet and one piece of cardboard.
3. Make available the different colored yarns to be used in the design.
4. Pass out the rest of the materials.
5. Show how to apply the yarn in concentric patterns on the skull.

Student Directions

1. Choose a color of yarn to start your design on the skull.
2. Apply glue on a section of the skull and begin to press down the yarn, working from the inside out. Use a pencil or stick to help position the yarn.

3. Continue designing the entire skull with either the same color yarn or different colors.
4. When finished, glue the skull to the piece of cardboard for support.

Hands-On Art Activities

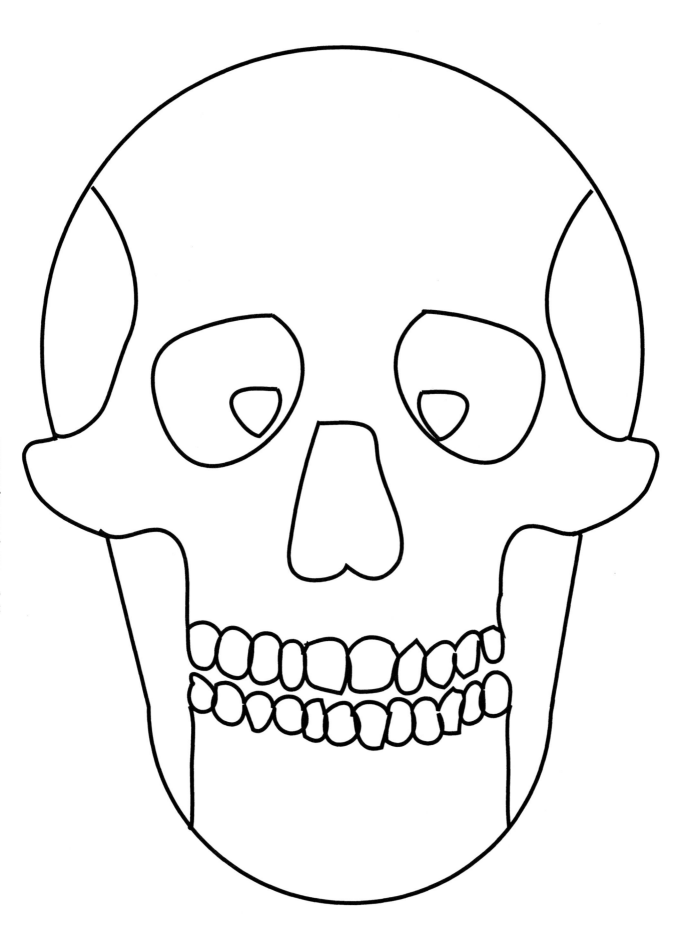

Thanksgiving

12. HARVEST CORN

Grade Level: K–3

The first Pilgrim mention of corn was in a letter written by Edward Winslow dated 1622. Corn was called "wheat" by the Pilgrims, and they soon came to rely on it, eating "about a peck of meal a week to a person"—over 4 cups a day. Corn was also a very important commodity to the Native Americans. It was their main flour source, and different parts of the plant were used to make many things, including eating utensils, pipes, bedding, and baskets.

Project Description

Students will use rolled tissue paper to create a corn-shaped pattern.

Advance Preparation

Bring in some real corn cobs to show the students (including some Indian corn, if available). Make a copy of the corn cob pattern sheet for each student. Have one 12" x 18" sheet of green tissue paper, two 12" x 18" sheets of yellow tissue paper, and one 6" x 12" piece of oak tag for each student.

Materials Needed

   12" x 18" sheets of green tissue paper
   12" x 18" sheets of yellow tissue paper
   6" x 12" sheets of oak tag
   Corn cob pattern sheets
   String
   Pencils
   Scissors
   White glue
   Real corn cobs

Connections to Other Disciplines

Social Studies: Discuss the origin of the Thanksgiving holiday and the importance of corn and other food sources at that time of American history.

34

Science: Discuss how corn is grown and harvested. Ask students: What is Indian corn?

Reading: Introduce *People of Corn: A Mayan Story* by Mary-Joan Gersen.

Cooking: Prepare plain corn kernels (canned, fresh, or frozen) or succotash and give your students a taste experience.

Teacher Directions

1. Show students the real corn cobs.
2. Give each student one 12" x 18" sheet of green tissue paper, two 12" x 18" sheets of yellow tissue paper, one 6" x 12" sheet of oak tag, and one corn cob pattern sheet.
3. Distribute the rest of the materials.

Student Directions

1. Trace the corn cob pattern onto the oak tag, then cut out the shape.
2. Cut the yellow tissue paper into small pieces and roll each piece into a small ball to make the kernels.
3. Glue the small yellow kernels onto the corn cob base. Let dry.
4. Cut the green tissue paper into three sections. These will be the husks.
5. Glue the husks to the back and sides of the corn cob. Let dry.
6. Pinch the ends of the husk and tie with string.

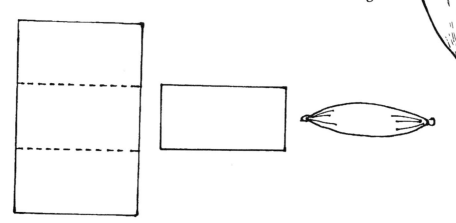

Variation

Instead of tissue-paper kernels, you can use real popcorn for kernels. Students can snack on popcorn, too!

13. FIRST THANKSGIVING DINNER

Grade Level: 1–3

The Pilgrims' first winter in Plymouth was a time of great hardship. The following summer, the Pilgrims were befriended by the Wampanoag, who taught them how to survive by planting and hunting. The first Thanksgiving was shared by the Pilgrims and the Wampanoag in the fall to celebrate a bountiful harvest.

Project Description

Students will use paper and magazine pictures to create a replica of the first Thanksgiving.

Advance Preparation

Collect oblong tissue boxes, one for each student, and enough cardboard to make benches around the tables. Have construction paper to decorate the tables. Make three copies of the Native Americans and Pilgrims pattern sheets for each student. Collect food magazines so students can cut out pictures of food.

Materials Needed

Empty oblong tissue boxes

Lightweight cardboard

Native Americans and Pilgrims pattern sheets

Markers or crayons

Scissors

Glue

Food magazines

Construction paper

Connections to Other Disciplines

Social Studies: What was the Wampanoag culture like? What was the Pilgrim culture like?

Critical thinking: Ask students how they would survive in a land that they knew nothing about with no modern conveniences.

Teacher Directions

1. Give each student an empty oblong tissue box and three copies of each of the Native Americans and Pilgrims pattern sheets.
2. Distribute the rest of the materials.

Student Directions

1. Cover your tissue box with construction paper and decorate it to look like a wooden table.
2. Think about what kinds of foods the Pilgrims and Native Americans would have eaten at that first Thanksgiving. Then look through the food magazines and cut out pictures of those foods.
3. Glue the pictures of the food to the table.
4. Make two benches for the table by cutting a 6" x 4" piece of cardboard. Create four sections by drawing lines an inch apart on the length of the cardboard. Then fold sections over to create a rectangular cube and tape together to create the bench.
5. Color the Pilgrims and Native Americans and cut them out. Fold along the lines indicated.
6. Glue the figures to the benches and let dry.

Hands-On Art Activities

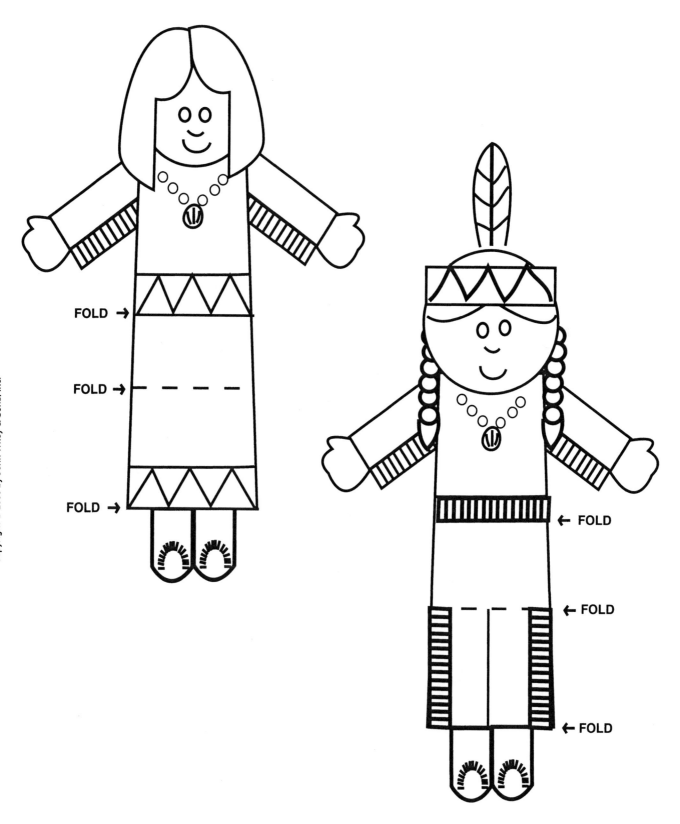

FOLD →

FOLD →

FOLD →

← FOLD

← FOLD

← FOLD

← FOLD

← FOLD

← FOLD

← FOLD

← FOLD

← FOLD

14. TURKEY MOSAIC

Grade Level: 2–3

Mosaic is an art form in which small pieces of colored glass, stone, or other materials are set in mortar. These pieces, each called a *tessera* (plural *tesserae*), are fitted together to form a picture.

Project Description

Students will use a mosaic to create a turkey pattern.

Advance Preparation

Collect many different colored seeds, grains, beans, and plant parts. Provide toothpicks or twigs, and cups to hold the mosaic pieces. Be sure to provide a thick craft glue. Make a copy of the turkey pattern sheet for each student. Use the turkey pattern to make a cardboard backing for each finished project.

Materials Needed

Turkey pattern sheets

Cardboard

Tesserae: seeds, grains, beans, plant parts, twigs

Thick white glue

Toothpicks or twigs to position the tesserae

Newspaper to cover work area

Sheets of paper to put under art to collect excess tesserae materials

Paper cups

Connections to Other Disciplines

Critical thinking/Aesthetic awareness: How do many things blend to appear as one? For example, many leaves on a tree are seen as one color.

Mathematics: Discuss the concept of *area*. How many pieces of each type of tessera does it take to fill in a section?

Science: Where did the tesserae used in the project come from? How can the different parts of plants be used?

Teacher Directions

1. Cover the work area with newspaper.
2. Fill each cup with one type of tessera (one type of seed in one cup, one type of grain in another cup, and so on).
3. Give a set of cups to each student, or give a group of students a set of cups to share.
4. Pass out glue and toothpicks for spreading the tesserae.
5. Give students extra paper to transfer excess seeds back to cups. Have an additional cup for mixed tesserae.
6. When projects are dry, glue them to cardboard backing for support.

Student Directions

1. Pick a kind of tessera to glue in one section of the turkey picture.
2. Cover the section with glue.
3. Put the tesserae on the glue and let stand one minute.
4. Hold up the turkey and gently sprinkle any excess pieces onto a piece of paper.
5. Pour the excess pieces back into their cup.
6. Pick another type of tesserae for another section of the turkey picture and glue it to that section.
7. Continue until all sections of the turkey have been filled in.
8. Allow the glue to dry thoroughly.

Hands-On Art Activities

15. TURKEY PINECONE MOBILE

Grade Level: 2–3

Mobiles are suspended sculptures with parts that can be moved by air currents. Alexander Calder (1898–1976) is credited with inventing the first mobile.

Project Description

Students will use decorated pinecones to create a turkey mobile.

Advance Preparation

For each student, collect at least three pinecones of the same size and a twig for hanging them, or have students find and bring in their own pinecones and twigs. The twig should be proportional to the size of the cones. Trim any branches off the twigs. Make one copy of the turkey body parts pattern for each student. Obtain string and glitter.

Materials Needed

Pinecones, 1" to 3" long

Twigs, 12" to 18" long

Turkey body parts pattern sheets

String

White glue

Tempera paints

Paint brushes

Water containers for cleanup

Scissors

Glitter

Newspaper to cover work area

Connections to Other Disciplines

Science: Discuss pinecones, their origin, and how they produce trees. Are there different kinds of pinecone shapes? What are the names of the trees that they come from? How does the mobile balance?

Social Studies: Discuss how pine trees and turkeys were used by the Pilgrims and the Native Americans.

Teacher Directions

1. Cover the work area with newspaper and put out water containers for cleaning brushes.
2. Give at least three pinecones, one twig, and one copy of the turkey parts pattern to each student.
3. Pass out the glue, glitter, paints, and brushes for decorating the pinecones.
4. Distribute the rest of the materials.

Student Directions

1. Decorate your pinecones with paint, glitter, or both.
2. Let the pinecones dry overnight.
3. Cut out the turkey heads and feet and glue them to your pinecones.
4. Tie a piece of string to each pinecone and then tie all three to the twig.
5. Tie a longer length of string to the middle of the twig to hang the mobile.

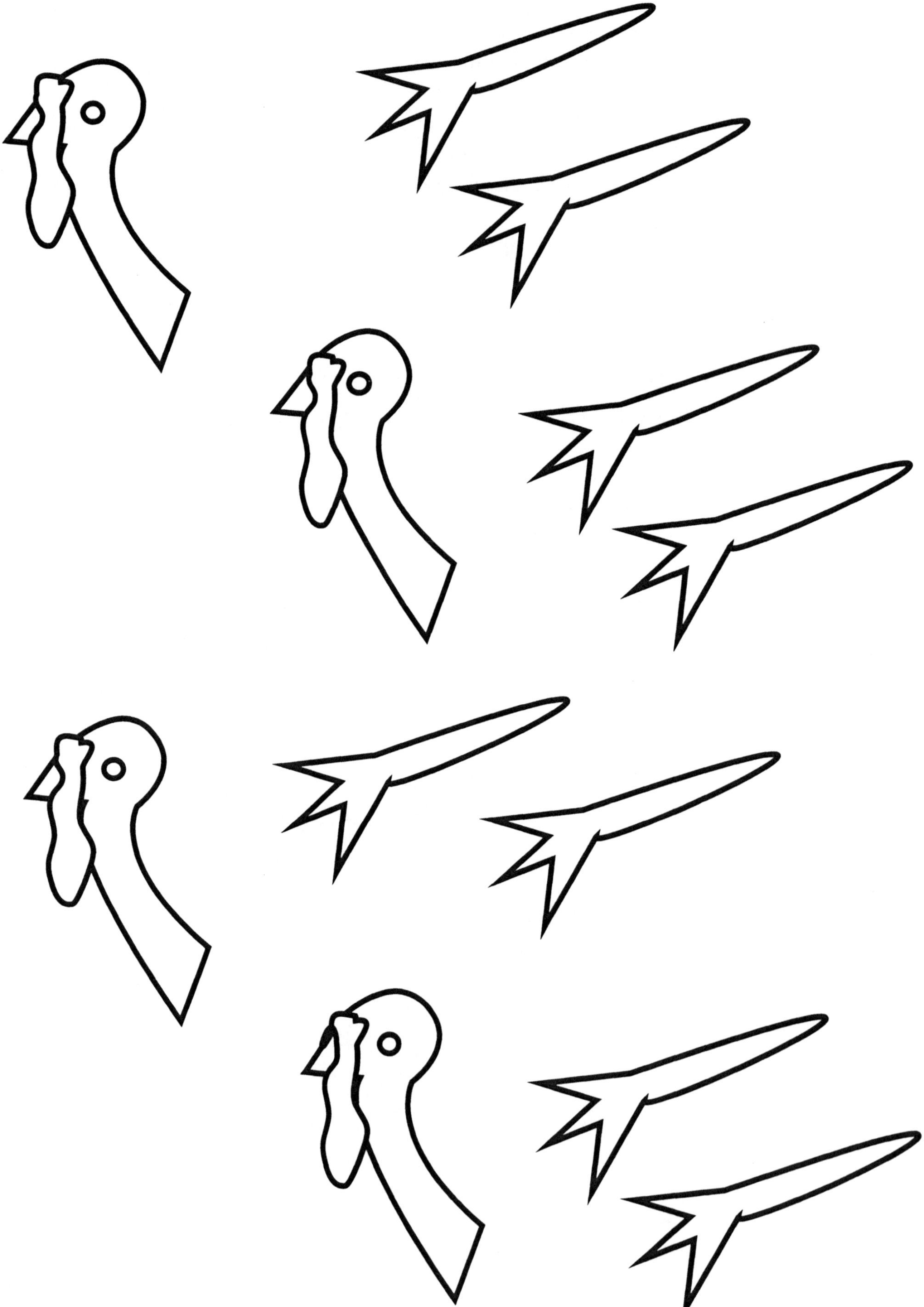

16. NATIVE AMERICAN CANOE

Grade Level: 2–3

The canoe was a major means of transportation for many Native Americans. They used canoes to move from place to place, to get to food sources, to fish, and to communicate with other tribes.

Project Description

Students will create Native American canoes from cut-out designs and then incorporate these canoes into a landscape mural. (*Note:* This project will be done in two lessons.)

Advance Preparation

Have available a 3' x 6' sheet of mural paper. You may want to partially fill in some of the river scene for the students to finish. Make one copy of the canoe pattern sheet for each student.

Materials Needed

> 3' x 6' sheet of mural paper
>
> Crayons or paints
>
> Canoe pattern sheets
>
> Masking tape
>
> Craft sticks

Connections to Other Disciplines

Music: Sing "This Land Is Your Land" by Woody Guthrie.

Social Studies: Introduce students to *Keepers of the Earth: Native American Stories and Environmental Activities* by Michael Caduto and Joseph Bruchak.

Reading: Introduce students to *America's Top 10 Rivers* by Jenny E. Tesar.

Science: Discuss the different river environments of the United States (Northeast, Central, Northwest).

Teacher Directions

Lesson 1

1. Discuss how Native Americans lived and how they used rivers and other waterways.
2. Give each student a canoe pattern sheet.
3. Distribute the rest of the materials.
4. Help students cut out and assemble their canoes.

Lesson 2

1. Help students create (or finish) the mural.
2. Have students tape their canoes to the mural.

Student Directions

Lesson 1

1. Color the canoe and the Native American.
2. Cut out the canoe and the Native American and fold along the fold lines.
3. Tape the Native American to the inside of the canoe.

Lesson 2

1. Along with your classmates, draw a river scene on the mural paper. Include trees and animals by the river.
2. Tape your canoe somewhere along the river. Use a craft stick for a paddle.

Hands-On Art Activities

FOLD

FOLD →

FOLD →

17. TRIBAL SHIELD

Grade Level: 3–4

Native American shields were used more for ritual than for protection. Tribal symbols were used in the shield designs. The materials most often used to make the shields were wood, bone, and leather.

Project Description

Students will create a shield using different Native American designs.

Advance Preparation

Cut one cardboard circle, 8" in diameter, for each student. Punch eight evenly spaced holes around the edge of each circle. Obtain yarn and beads and purchase feathers from a craft store or authorized seller of domestic bird feathers. Have on hand paints, brushes, and cups, as well as cleanup materials. Collect pictures of traditional Native American shield designs.

Materials Needed

  8" diameter cardboard circles

  Hole punch

  Yarn, feathers, and beads

  Pencils

  Paints

  Paintbrushes

  Cups of water

  Newspaper to cover work area

Connections to Other Disciplines

Social Studies: Ask students how different tribal shields might have reflected where particular tribes lived.

Mathematics: Explore symmetry and pattern.

Teacher Directions

1. Discuss Native American culture and the purpose of tribal shields.
2. Show pictures of shields from different Native American tribes as well as the Native American symbols shown here.
3. Cover the work area with newspaper.
4. Give each student one 8" diameter cardboard circle.
5. Explain how to draw designs on the shields in a symmetrical pattern.
6. Help students weave the yarn and attach the feathers and beads to the shield.

Student Directions

1. Look at the Native American designs and draw one or more on the cardboard circle.
2. Paint your design.
3. Use yarn to weave through the holes around the shield and to attach feathers and beads to the shield.

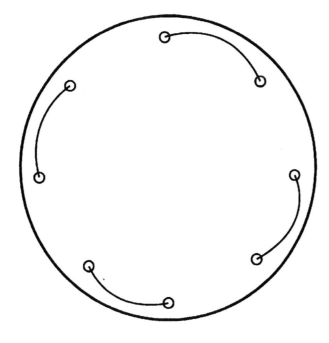

Threading Shield

Native American Symbols

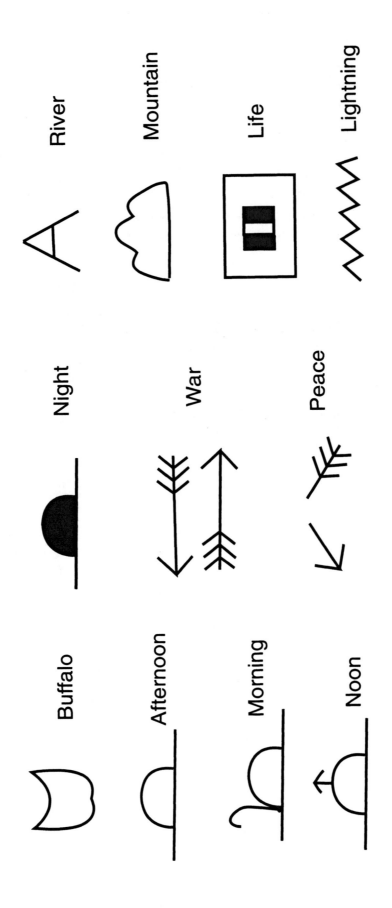

Buffalo

Afternoon

Morning

Noon

Night

War

Peace

River

Mountain

Life

Lightning

18. TOTEM POLE

Grade Level: 3–4

Totem poles are created by some Native Americans, particularly those in the Northwest. The word *totem* applies to animals or spirits that symbolize the connection to a higher force. The pole is decorated by carving animals and symbols around a tree. Then the pole is positioned in a sacred location where the Native Americans can commune with ancestors and animal spirit guides.

Project Description

Students will create a totem pole of animals and facial features using paper towel rolls and colored paper.

Advance Preparation

Collect, or have students collect, enough empty paper towel rolls so that each student has one. Make one copy of the body parts pattern sheet for each student. Find examples of various Native American totem poles.

Materials Needed

    Empty paper towel rolls

    Construction paper in different colors

    Scissors

    Colored pencils or crayons

    White glue

    Body parts pattern sheets

Connections to Other Disciplines

Reading: Introduce *Totem Pole* by Diane Hoyt-Goldsmith.

Social Studies: How do Native Americans of the Northwest create their totem poles from large trees? Why are animal and spirit symbols so important to Native Americans?

Language Arts: Can you think of a story to go with your totem pole?

Teacher Directions

1. Discuss Native American totem poles and show examples.
2. Give each student a paper towel roll, one body parts pattern sheet, and sheets of different colored construction paper.
3. Help students to trace the patterns on the construction paper and cut them out.
4. Help students fold the body parts and glue them to their totem poles.

Student Directions

1. Look at the animals and other carvings on the totem pole examples. Think of how you want to design your own totem pole.
2. Cut the body part patterns out of the pattern sheet.
3. Trace the body part patterns onto different colors of construction paper and cut them out. Fill in details with colored pencils or crayons.
4. Glue the cut-out body parts to the paper towel roll to complete your totem pole.

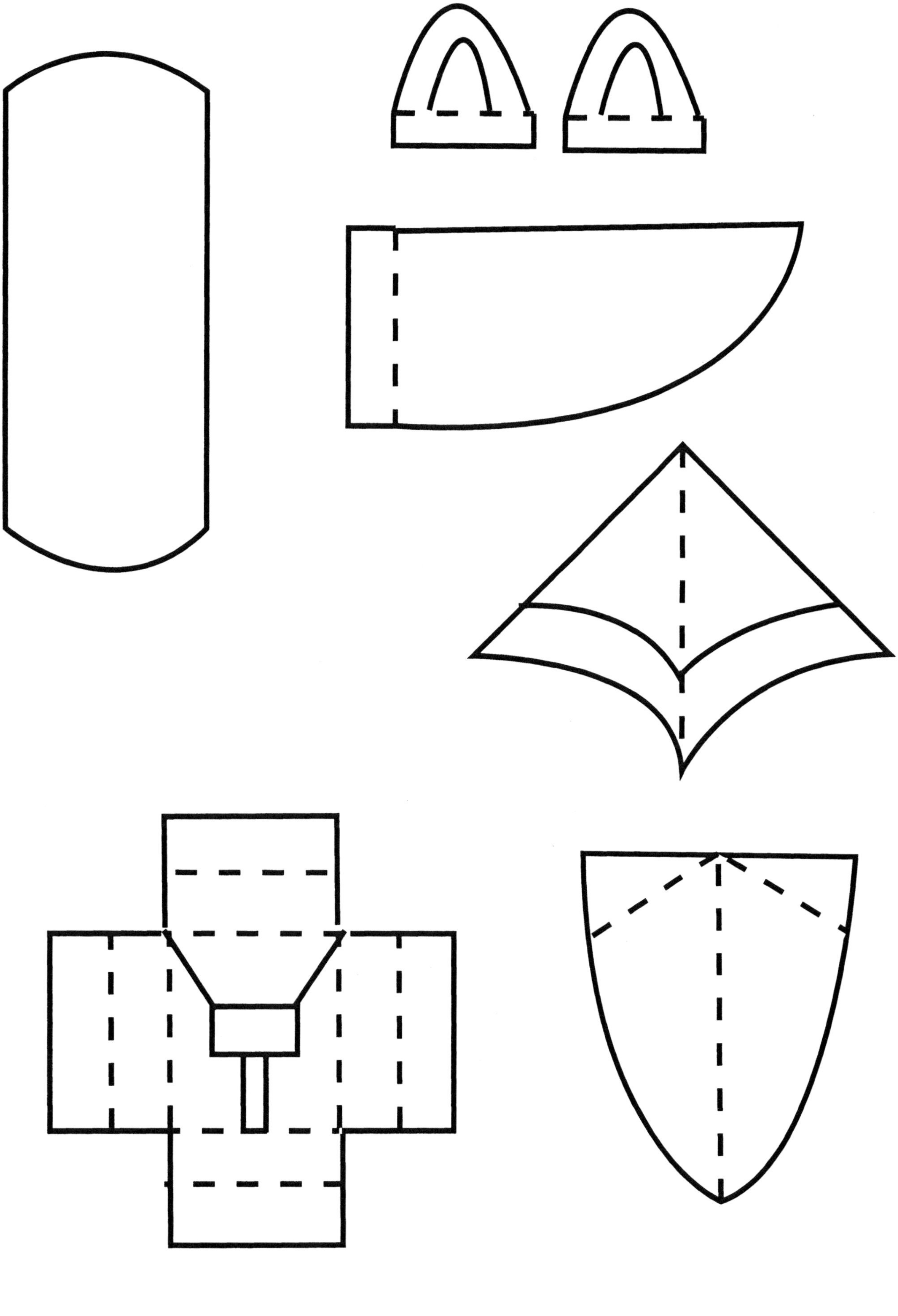

Winter

GIMEL

HE

General

19. MARSHMALLOW SNOWMAN

Grade Level: K–1

Here is a fun, creative way to make a winter decoration.

Project Description

Students will create a snowman using marshmallows. (CAUTION: Be sure your students do not eat the glued marshmallows.)

Advance Preparation

Have yarn and black, red, and orange construction paper, and collect small twigs or toothpicks and small stones, peppercorns, or black-oil sunflower seeds for the facial features. Make a basic snowman-and-sled sculpture for each student: use a glue gun to glue two marshmallows together. (CAUTION: Be sure only an adult uses the glue gun.) Cut 3" x 8" strips of corrugated cardboard (cutting the long side across the grain). Use a glue gun to attach the marshmallows to the cardboard. Curl up the front of the cardboard to make a toboggan shape. Cut one 1/2" x 9" strip of felt for each student.

Materials Needed

Marshmallows

Corrugated cardboard

Glue gun (CAUTION: To be used by an adult only)

Different colored pieces of felt

Small twigs or toothpicks

Black, red, and orange construction paper

Scissors

White glue

Yarn

Small stones, peppercorns, or black-oil sunflower seeds (unhulled)

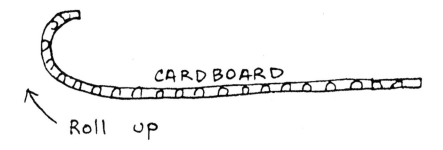

CARDBOARD

Roll up

Connections to Other Disciplines

Reading: Introduce *The Snowman* by Raymond Briggs and *The Snowman Who Went for a Walk* by Mira Lobe.

Science: Discuss what marshmallows are made from.

Cooking: Let your students snack on marshmallows. How about making hot cocoa with marshmallows in the classroom, or crisped-rice cereal and marshmallow bars?

Teacher Directions

1. Give each student one of the snowman-and-sled sculptures you have prepared and a 1/2" x 9" strip of felt.
2. Hand out the rest of the materials.
3. Help students tie the scarves around their snowmen.
4. Help students cut and glue on the facial features (circles and triangles) and the yarn handle.

Student Directions

1. Carefully tie the scarf around the snowman's neck.
2. Gently insert the two twigs or toothpicks for arms.
3. Cut circles and triangles out of construction paper to make facial features for your snowman. Glue these on.
4. Tie yarn around the snowman's hands and glue the middle to the front of the sled to make a handle.
5. Display your snowman along with your classmates' snowmen in the classroom.

20. PENGUINS AT PLAY

Grade Level: K–1

Penguins are flightless birds that love the cold weather. This fun winter activity also features the interesting effect of using salt with watercolors.

Project Description

Students will create standing penguins using paper, watercolors, and salt.

Advance Preparation

Use the pattern and 8" x 10" sheets of oak tag to make a penguin shape for each student. Cut a 3" square piece of orange construction paper and obtain a sheet of 24" square oak tag for each student. Put salt in small cups.

Materials Needed

Penguin pattern sheets

8" x 10" sheets of oak tag

Orange construction paper

Black paint

Orange paint

Blue watercolors

Paintbrushes

Salt

Small cups

24" square sheets of white oak tag

Newspaper to cover work area

Connections to Other Disciplines

Science: Locate the places where penguins live in the wild on a world map or globe. Have any students seen penguins at a zoo?

Language Arts: Have students talk about the appearance of different kinds of penguins. Why do they think penguins are referred to as "little gentlemen"?

Reading: Introduce *Little Penguin's Tale* by Audrey Wood.

Teacher Directions

1. Cover the work area with newspaper.
2. Give each student an oak tag penguin shape, a 3" square of orange construction paper, a 24" square sheet of oak tag, and a small cup of salt.
3. Distribute the other materials.
4. Help students with gluing and painting.

Student Directions

1. Use black paint to color the outer body of the penguin except for the feet.
2. Paint the penguin's feet orange. Let dry.
3. Fold the small orange paper square in half to form a triangle. Glue one side of the triangle to the penguin for the beak.
4. Take the large sheet of white oak tag and draw a wavy line across the middle of the paper.
5. Paint the bottom half of the large sheet of oak tag with blue watercolors for the ocean, then sprinkle some salt onto the blue watercolor paint before the paint dries. Let dry.
6. Fold and crease the penguin's feet so that the penguin is standing.
7. Put glue on the bottoms of the feet, and glue the penguin to the beach on the ocean picture.

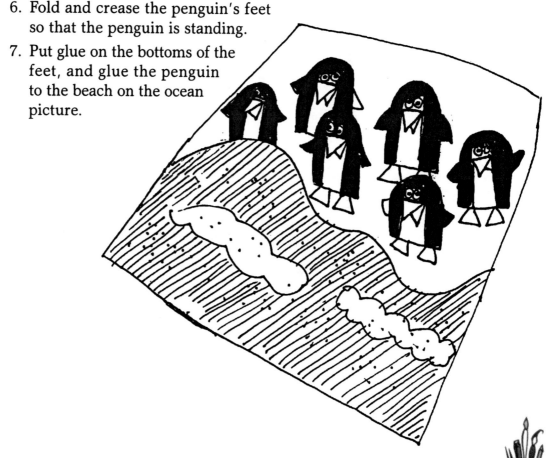

21. Three-Dimensional Snowman Family

Grade Level: 1–3
Make a cheerful family of snowmen to brighten up the winter season.

Project Description
Students will create a three-dimensional paper snowman family.

Advance Preparation
Have one paper plate for each student and enough oak tag for each student to make several snowmen.

Materials Needed
White oak tag
Paper plates
Scissors
Markers
Glue

Connections to Other Disciplines
Social Studies: People live in social groups called families. Discuss how many members are in the students' families. (*Note:* Be sensitive to the children's specific situations.)

Science: Discuss snow. How is it formed? Some children may never have seen snow because of where they live, so how might they be able to make "snow" in the classroom? (Perhaps use shaved ice?)

Reading: Introduce *All Kinds of Families* by Noima Simon.

Teacher Directions
1. Give each student a paper plate and a few sheets of white oak tag.
2. Distribute the rest of the materials.
3. Help students draw the snowman shape, if necessary.
4. Help with the cutting and assembling.

Student Directions

1. Think of how many people are in your family at home. You will need a snowman for each person.

2. Draw the snowmen shapes on the oak tag. Include a tab at the bottom of each snowman that you can fold over to make a base. Your teacher will help you, if needed.

3. Color your snowmen using markers.

4. Cut out each snowman.

5. Fold each snowman at the base, and put some glue on the base.

6. Glue each snowman onto the paper plate so that it stands.

Optional: Draw, color, and cut out trees to add to your family scene.

22. SLED RIDE

Grade Level: 2–3

Before cars were invented, many people used to ride on horse-drawn sleighs to travel along wintry paths. Nowadays, you see children of all ages sliding downhill on sleds.

Project Description

Students will create a winter scene with moving figures on sleds.

Advance Preparation

Make a copy of the sled riders pattern for each student. Obtain craft sticks and sheets of 12" x 18" white paper (one for each student).

Materials Needed

Sled riders pattern sheets

12" x 18" sheets of white paper

Craft sticks

Crayons

Scissors

Glue

Connections to Other Disciplines

Social Studies: Discuss where in the world people might still use sleds as a form of transportation. Do students know anything about the Iditarod?

Science: Discuss friction. Why is sledding on snow easy? What about skating on ice?

Reading: Introduce *Mush! Across Alaska in the World's Longest Sled-Dog Race* by Patricia Seibert and *Aklak: A Tale from the Iditarod* by Robert J. Blake.

Teacher Directions

1. Give each student a copy of the sled riders pattern sheet and a sheet of 12" x 18" white paper.
2. Distribute the rest of the materials.
3. Help students as needed.

Student Directions

1. Draw two overlapping mountains on your paper.

2. Draw an additional mountain or two in the distance.

3. Draw small and large trees for perspective.

4. Cut a slit inside the picture along the edge of one of the mountains. Leave about 2" from each edge of the paper.

5. Color the two sled riders on the pattern sheet.

6. Cut out the two riders.

7. Glue one rider to the end of a craft stick.

8. Glue the other rider to the back of the first rider. Let dry.

9. Insert the stick through the slit on the scene and let your rider sled along the mountain.

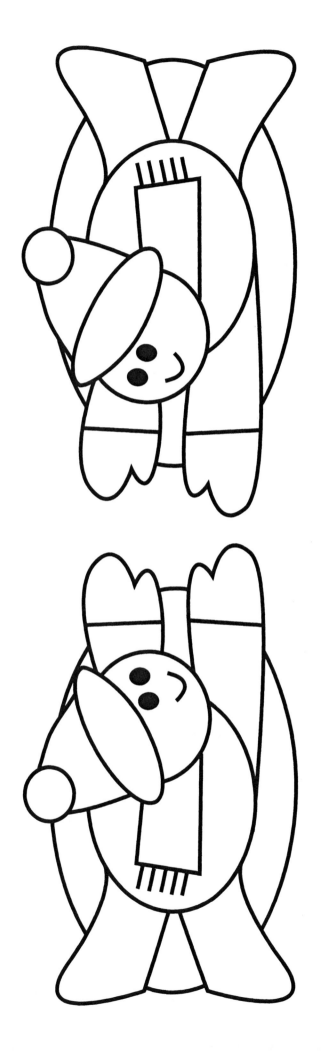

23. SNOWFLAKE

Grade Level: 2–4

Snowflakes are made of water in the atmosphere that has frozen and crystallized into geometric shapes. The structure of the snowflake starts from the center and develops outward. Each snowflake is different from all the rest and all are perfectly symmetrical.

Project Description

Students will fold and cut paper to create snowflakes.

Advance Preparation

Cut or buy 9" squares of white paper so there are several squares for each student. Prepare several finished snowflakes to show the class.

Materials Needed

9" square sheets of white construction paper

Scissors

Tape

Connections to Other Disciplines

Mathematics: Discuss the symmetrical shape and number of sides of snowflakes.

Science: Discuss how snowflakes are created in the atmosphere. Discuss different types of crystals.

Reading: Introduce *In the Flaky Frost Morning* by Karla Kuskin and *Snow Day* by Moira Fain.

Teacher Directions

1. Display several examples of the cutout snowflakes.
2. Give each student several 9" squares of white construction paper.
3. Distribute the rest of the materials.
4. Help students with the folding and cutting as necessary.

Student Directions

1. Fold your square in half, from the top right point to the bottom left point, to form a triangle.
2. Fold this triangle in half again to form a smaller triangle.
3. Fold this small triangle in half again to form a smaller triangle.
4. Cut out a V shape, leaving about 1" from the edges.
5. Now cut out small triangles or scallops along the outside and inside edges.
6. Open up your snowflake and tape it to the wall.
7. Now make another snowflake that's different from the first.

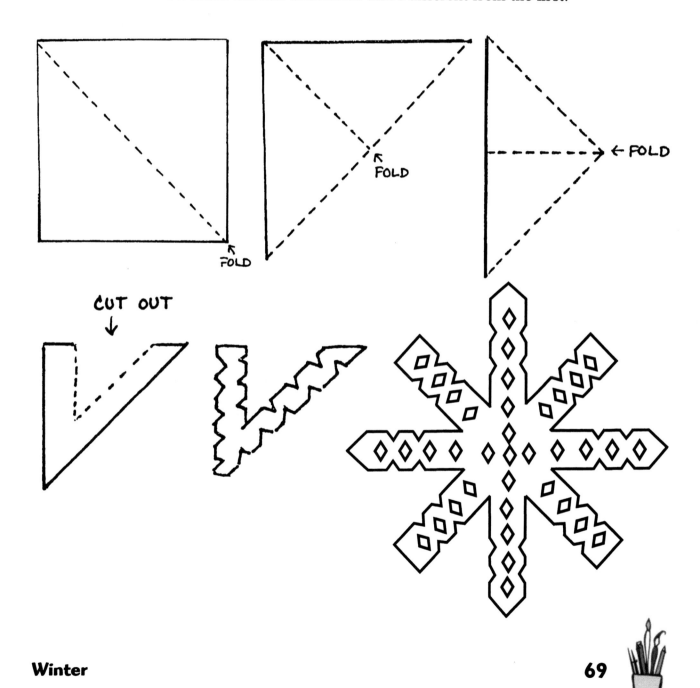

24. TOBOGGAN RIDE

Grade Level: 2–4

The toboggan is a sled that was first used by northern Native Americans to transport items over snow-covered areas. In the twentieth century tobogganing became a popular winter sport and bobsledding is even part of the Winter Olympic Games.

Project Description

Students will create a toboggan with two riders using paper and patterns.

Advance Preparation

Make one copy of the toboggan riders pattern sheet for each student. Cut out 4" x 12" strips of oak tag for the toboggans.

Materials Needed

Toboggan riders pattern sheets

Crayons

Scissors

Glue

Oak tag

Pencils

String

Connections to Other Disciplines

Social Studies: Discuss various events of the Winter Olympic Games, including the bobsled competition. How long have sleds been a part of the Olympics?

Reading: Introduce *Eskimo Boy: Life in an Inupiaq Eskimo Village* by Russ Kendall and *Dashing Through the Snow: The Story of the Jr. Iditarod* by Sherry Shahan.

Teacher Directions

1. Give each student one copy of the toboggan riders pattern sheet and a 4" x 12" oak tag strip.
2. Distribute the rest of the materials.
3. Help students fold and glue the riders.
4. Help students curl the oak tag toboggan.

Student Directions

1. Color the two riders for the toboggan.
2. Cut out the riders.
3. Fold the riders' legs forward so that the riders are "sitting."
4. Spread some glue on the back of each rider's legs and place the riders on the strip of oak tag so that one rider is behind the other.
5. Fold the riders' arms so that the back rider's arms are on the front rider's shoulders.
6. Use a pencil to curl the front of the oak tag toboggan.
7. Cut string to use as a handle for the front rider to hold, and glue the string to the rider's hands.

How might you and your classmates "race" your toboggans?

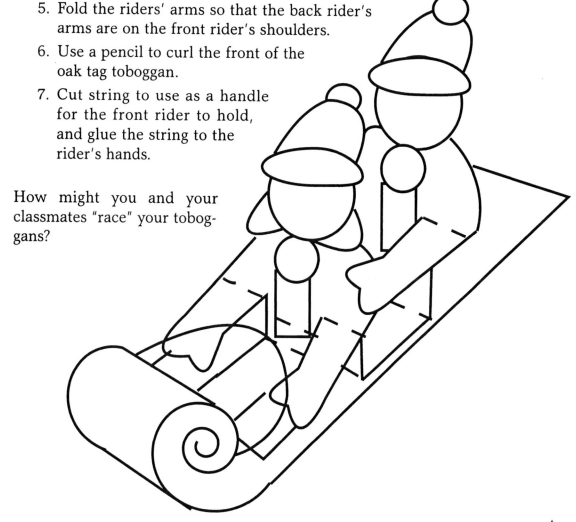

25. BEAR FAMILY HOUSE

Grade Level: 3–4

Bears can weigh up to 1,700 pounds, measure up to ten feet long, and live to be as old as thirty. Bears live in different habitats, ranging from mountains and forests to arctic ice and snow. They hibernate in dens during the winter, going without food for three to five months.

Project Description

Students will create a bears' house, or den, that shows the front of the house and the bears inside.

Advance Preparation

Get enough sheets of 12" x 18" white drawing paper to give one to each student.

Materials Needed

12" x 18" sheets of white drawing paper
Crayons

Connections to Other Disciplines

Science: Explain hibernation and how bears can survive without food for such a long time.

Social Studies: Discuss how Native Americans and settlers hunted bears for food and clothing.

Cooking: Most bears like to eat berries and honey. Bring in different kinds of berries (strawberries, raspberries, blueberries, boysenberries, and so on) and different flavors of honey (clover, orange blossom, and so on) for students to sample.

Reading: Introduce *The Biggest Bear* by Lynn Ward, *Alaska's Three Bears* by Shelley Gill, and *Do Bears Sleep All Winter? Questions and Answers About Bears* by Melvin and Gilda Berger.

Teacher Directions

1. Draw on the chalkboard the steps for drawing a sleeping bear (see the illustrations).
2. Give each student a 12" x 18" sheet of white drawing paper and some crayons.
3. Help students draw the sleeping bears.

Hands-On Art Activities

Student Directions

1. Fold your sheet of paper in half.

2. With the fold at the top, draw the bears' house on the front of the paper. Create a nighttime scene.

3. Open the paper. Think of how many people live in your house, including yourself. Now draw that same number of bears sleeping. Use the entire inside of the paper, if necessary, to fit your bears. Follow the diagrams on the chalkboard for how to draw a sleeping bear.

4. Finish the bears' house by coloring in the nighttime scene and the sleeping bears.

BEAR FAMILY HOUSE

Hands-On Art Activities

26. POP-UP WINTER LANDSCAPE

Grade Level: 3–5

A winter landscape offers a good opportunity to discuss perspective and show how it can be created with different sized background and foreground shapes.

Project Description

Students will create a three-dimensional winter landscape.

Advance Preparation

Have at least three sheets of white construction paper for each student.

Materials Needed

White construction paper

Scissors

Glue

Markers

Connections to Other Disciplines

Science: Discuss the horizon and focal point.

Social Studies: Discuss the living conditions in cold, snowy areas of the world, such as Alaska and the tundra regions. How would living in those areas compare with where the students live?

Reading: Introduce *The Igloo* by Charlotte and David Yue and *Who Lives in the Arctic?* by Susan Canizares and Pamela Chanko.

Teacher Directions

1. Discuss how the size and position of objects can indicate perspective.
2. Give each student three pieces of white construction paper.
3. Distribute the rest of the materials.
4. Help students as needed.

Student Directions

1. Fold one sheet of paper in half.
2. Make four cuts at the fold, going 1" into the paper.
3. Open the paper into an L shape and push a cut section in the opposite direction.

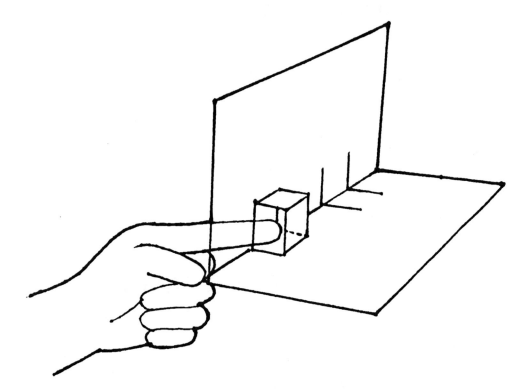

4. On the back half of the folded paper, draw overlapping mountains.
5. On another sheet of paper, draw small, medium, and large fir trees.
6. Color the trees.
7. Cut out the trees.
8. Glue the smaller trees at the top of the mountains.

Hands-On Art Activities

9. Glue the medium trees at the bottom of the mountains.
10. Fold a small piece of paper in half and glue it to the back of a large tree.
11. Glue a large tree in front of the scene.
12. Glue another large tree to one of the pop-up boxes you created.
13. On the third sheet of paper, draw a house.
14. Color the house.
15. Cut out the house and glue it to the other pop-up box.

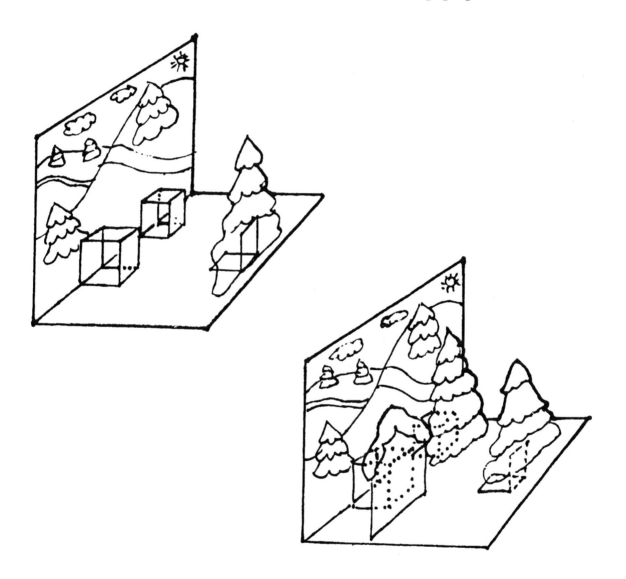

Hanukkah

27. MENORAH

Grade Level: 2–3

Hanukkah is the Jewish Festival of Lights, which celebrates the victory of the Maccabees, a group of rebels fighting for religious freedom, over Greek forces. During the festival, at the end of each day a candle is lit from a group of eight candles in a candleholder called the *menorah*. A ninth candle, called the *shamash,* is used to light the others. The menorah represents a lamp in the Jewish temple that had only one day's worth of oil in it, but that miraculously burned for eight days.

Project Description

Students will create a menorah using paper towel and toilet paper rolls and tissue paper.

Advance Preparation

Each student will need one paper towel roll and eight toilet paper rolls. Cut 2" squares of yellow tissue paper and orange tissue paper. (Each student will need nine of each color.) Bring examples of menorahs in to show the class.

Materials Needed

Paper towel rolls

Toilet paper rolls

Yellow and orange tissue paper

Tape

Glue

Paints

Paintbrushes

Newspaper to cover work area

Connections to Other Disciplines

Reading: Introduce *Festival of Lights* by Maida Silverman and *Hanukkah* by Alan Benjamin.

Science: Discuss why flames can be seen in various shades of yellow, orange, red, and even blue.

Cooking: Explain that potato latkes (pancakes) are a traditional Jewish dish often served during Hanukkah. You may want to make and serve them to your students.

Teacher Directions

1. Explain the history of Hanukkah and the menorah and show examples of menorahs to the class.
2. Cover the work area with newspaper.
3. Distribute one paper towel roll and eight toilet paper rolls to each student.
4. Hand out the rest of the materials.
5. Help students connect the cardboard tubes.

Student Directions

1. Paint your cardboard tubes, either in different colors or all the same color. Let dry.
2. Position four of the smaller tubes on each side of the longer tube and tape the sides to each other at the top and bottom. Use glue to attach the two smaller ones on either side of the longer tube.
3. Crumple a square of yellow tissue paper and orange tissue paper to make a flame shape, and insert into the top of each candle.

28. DREIDEL

Grade Level: 2–4

During Hanukkah, a game for good luck is played with a dreidel. A dreidel has four sides on which are written symbols that spell out "A great miracle happened there." In the game, the dreidel is spun like a top.

Project Description

Students will make a dreidel out of a milk carton and play a traditional game.

Advance Preparation

Collect a small milk carton for each student. Clean and let dry, then tape the opening shut. Have a new, unsharpened pencil or a dowel for each student. Draw the four symbols (*nun, gimel, he,* and *shin*) on the chalkboard.

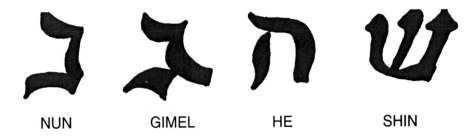

NUN   GIMEL   HE   SHIN

Materials Needed

    Clean, empty small milk cartons

    Construction paper in various light colors

    Glue

    Scissors

    Unsharpened pencils or dowels

    Small tokens for the game

    Crayons or markers

Connections to Other Disciplines

Science: Discuss how a top works. Why does it balance while spinning and then topple?

Social Studies: What is the historical significance of the traditions followed on Hanukkah?

Reading: Introduce *The Very Best Hanukkah Gift* by Joanne Rocklin, *Our Eight Nights of Hanukkah* by Michael J. Rosen, and *The Magic Dreidels* by Eric A. Kimmel.

Teacher Directions

1. Give each student a milk carton and a pencil.
2. Distribute the rest of the materials.
3. Help students cut the paper to the right size to fit over the milk carton's sides.
4. Explain the meanings of the four symbols on the chalkboard and that they'll be used to play the dreidel game.
5. Help students punch holes for the pencil.

Student Directions

1. Trace around the milk carton and cut pieces of construction paper to fit over each side of the carton.
2. Glue the pieces of paper to the sides of the carton.
3. Use crayons or markers to write and draw the symbols that are shown on the chalkboard on the sides of the carton, one symbol per side.
4. Your teacher will help you punch a hole at the top and bottom of your dreidel. Then insert the pencil as shown.

Dreidel Game Directions (for three or four players)

1. Put small tokens in the middle of the table. This is the "pot."
2. The first player spins the dreidel. When the dreidel comes to rest, the letter showing tells that player what he or she has earned. *Nun* is "you get nothing"; *gimel* is "you take the whole pot"; *he* is "you take half of the pot"; and *shin* is "you must put one token back into the pot."
3. The game continues with the next player spinning the dreidel.
4. The player with the most tokens at the end of game time is the winner.

Christmas

29. TREE STENCIL

Grade Level: K–3
Decorating trees for Christmas dates back to the sixteenth century in Germany. The stencil in this project can be used to make Christmas cards or used for seasonal designs.

Project Description
Students will make patterns with a tree stencil and watercolors.

Advance Preparation
Make a copy of the tree pattern sheet for each student. Get enough sheets of 10" x 15" watercolor paper so that each student has at least one. Have watercolors, paintbrushes, and fine-line markers for the students.

Materials Needed
Tree pattern sheets
10" x 15" sheets of watercolor paper
Tape
Watercolors
Paintbrushes
Fine-line markers
Scissors
Newspaper to cover work area

Connections to Other Disciplines
Social Studies: Discuss and show examples of how stencil designs, patterns, and borders are used on furniture, walls, and household items in many cultures.

Science: Explore the color spectrum. What colors are made when certain colors are overlapped?

Language Arts: Have students pretend they are living during colonial times in U.S. history. How might they have celebrated Christmas?

84

Teacher Directions

1. Show students a sample or two of how to make a stencil print on paper.
2. Cover the work area with newspaper.
3. Give each student a tree pattern sheet and a sheet of 10" x 15" watercolor paper.
4. Distribute the rest of the materials.
5. Help students as needed.

Student Directions

1. Cut out your tree pattern.
2. Attach the pattern to the paper using a very small piece of tape.
3. Gently brush watercolor paint across the pattern onto the paper. Let dry.
4. Carefully remove the tape and pattern to show the stenciled outline of the tree.
5. Use a fine-line marker to draw short lines on the tree stencil, as shown.
6. Overlap this painted tree with the tree pattern and repeat the pattern using a different color of watercolor. What happens to the colors?

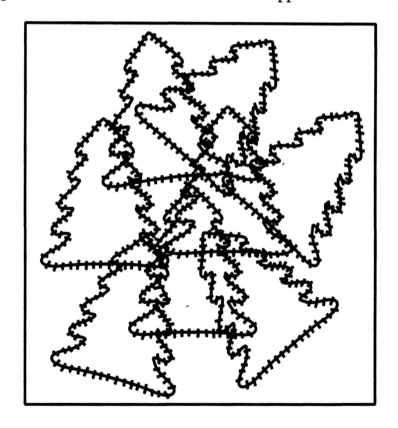

30. SANTA'S NIGHTTIME VISIT

Grade Level: K–3

In "The Night Before Christmas"—attributed to Clement C. Moore—Santa Claus, or St. Nick, is imagined flying over the rooftops in his reindeer-drawn sleigh. Here's a creative project that recreates the scene with a city backdrop.

Project Description

Students will create a nighttime cityscape with Santa.

Advance Preparation

Buy sheets of 12" x 18" construction paper in blue and black (enough to give one to each student). Make a finished sample of the project to show students. Bring in "The Night Before Christmas."

Materials Needed

12" x 18" sheets of blue construction paper

12" x 18" sheets of black construction paper

Chalk

Crayons

Scissors

Glue

Connections to Other Disciplines

Social Studies: Discuss how Santa Claus is depicted in different parts of the world.

Language Arts: Discuss "The Night Before Christmas" and various kinds of poetry (haiku, blank verse, and so on).

Reading: Introduce *Who's That Knocking on Christmas Eve?* by Jan Brett and *Santa Claus, Inc.* by Linda Ford.

Teacher Directions

1. Read "The Night Before Christmas" by Clement C. Moore.
2. Show your finished example of the cityscape.
3. Give each student one black and one blue sheet of paper.
4. Distribute the rest of the materials.
5. Help students as needed.

Student Directions

1. Use white chalk to draw a city skyline on black paper.
2. Cut out the skyline and glue the black skyline onto the blue paper.

3. Use chalk to draw windows and doors on the black buildings.
4. Now draw Santa Claus in his sled and his reindeer. They should be flying in the sky over your city buildings.
5. Finish your cityscape with snowflakes.

Hands-On Art Activities

31. TISSUE-BALL WREATH

Grade Level: 1–3

Like Christmas trees, wreaths and other evergreen boughs have traditionally been brought indoors for holidays as a symbol of everlasting life. Even as early as ancient Roman times, wreaths of holly were exchanged during a holiday honoring the god Saturn.

Project Description

Students will create wreaths using large paper plates and tissue paper.

Advance Preparation

Cut out 3" squares of green and red tissue paper. Bring in a large paper plate and a red bow for each student, and green construction paper if using the variation. Make a sample of a finished wreath to show students.

Materials Needed

Large paper plates

Scissors

3" squares of green tissue paper

3" squares of red tissue paper

White glue

Red bows

Green construction paper (optional)

Connections to Other Disciplines

Social Studies: Discuss the historical significance of wreaths.

Teacher Directions

1. Display a finished wreath for the students.
2. Give each student a paper plate and a bow.
3. Distribute the rest of the materials.
4. Show students how to cut out the center hole from the paper plate.

Student Directions

1. Fold the paper plate in half and cut out a half circle along the fold. Open up the plate.

2. Crumple green squares of tissue paper into small balls to cover your plates. Attach each one to the plate with glue.

3. Glue a crumpled red tissue-paper ball to give a holly-berry appearance to different areas of the green-covered wreath.

4. Glue a red bow to your wreath to complete the look!

Variation

1. Have each student trace his or her hand twenty-five times on green construction paper.

2. Help students to cut out these handprints.

3. Have students cut out the paper plate as described earlier, and have them glue their handprints onto the paper plate.

4. Have students glue on crumpled red tissue-paper balls to give a holly-berry appearance, and finish the wreath with a glued-on red bow.

32. ANGEL ORNAMENT

Grade Level: 2–3

Angels are found in nearly all religious traditions. Angels are particularly associated with Christmas because of the angels who announced the birth of Jesus. Angels are believed to help people in critical situations.

Project Description

Students will create an angel ornament.

Advance Preparation

Make a copy of the angel pattern for each student. Cut one 6" piece of oak tag for each student. Cut different colors of tissue paper into 2" squares.

Materials Needed

Angel pattern sheets

Oak tag

Tissue paper in different colors

Pipe cleaners

Scissors

Glue

Connections to Other Disciplines

Social Studies: Discuss folklore from different parts of the world. What beliefs do different cultures celebrate at Christmas and the New Year?

Teacher Directions

1. Give each student a copy of the angel pattern sheet and an oak tag square.
2. Distribute the rest of the materials.
3. Help students as needed.

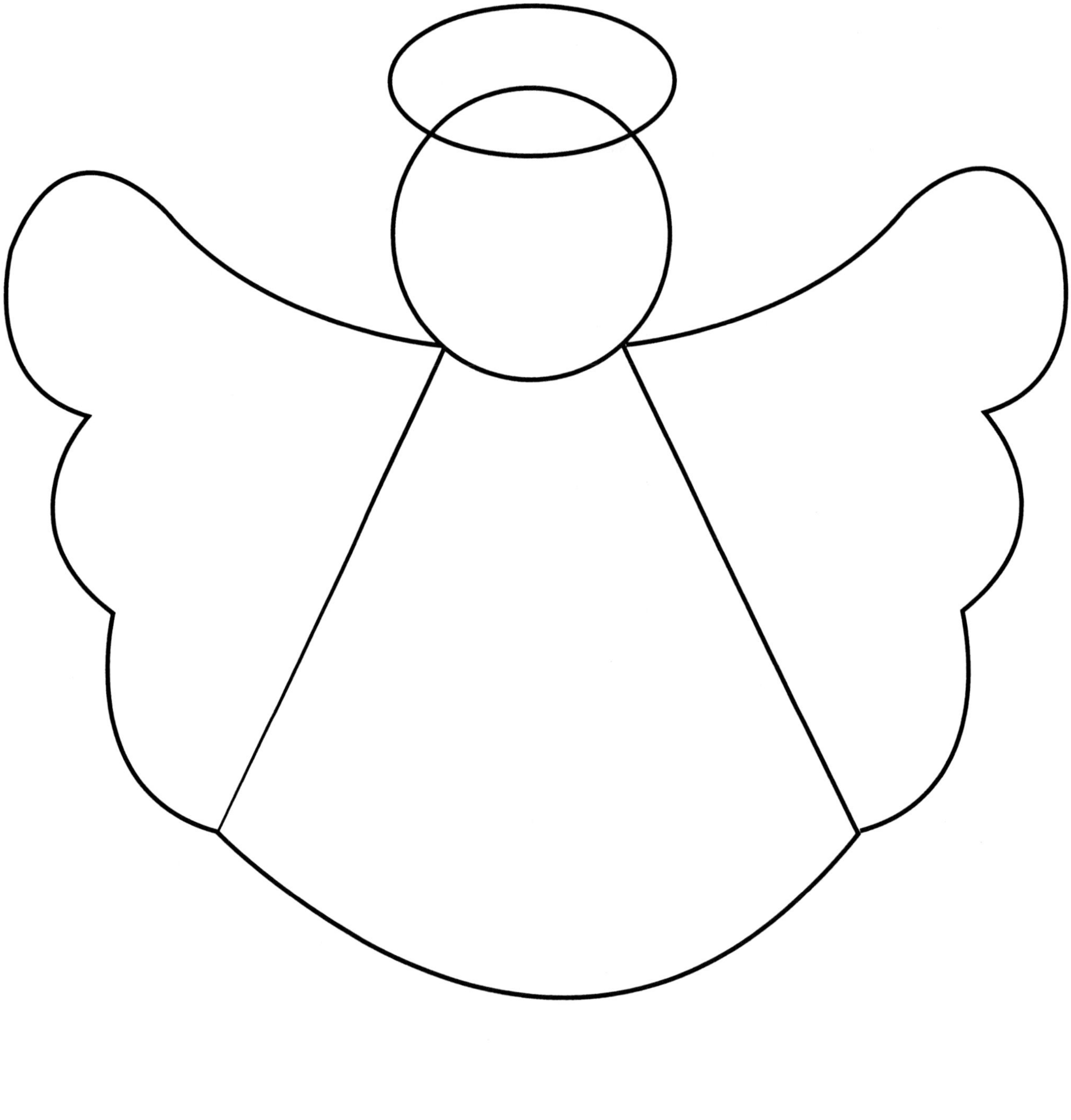

Student Directions

1. Cut out the angel pattern.
2. Trace the pattern onto the oak tag and cut out.
3. Roll up 2" squares of different colored tissue paper into balls.
4. Glue the tissue paper balls onto the angel to cover all the areas. Let dry.
5. Form a pipe cleaner into a circle and glue it to the angel's head as a halo.
6. Use another pipe cleaner as a hook to hang your finished angel on a Christmas tree or in the classroom.

33. HOLIDAY BELL

Grade Level: 2–4

The custom of ringing bells during the holidays began as a way to drive away evil spirits.

Project Description

Students will use a Styrofoam cup and colorful cereal to create a holiday bell.

Advance Preparation

Bring to class two boxes of colorful cereal O's and small paper cups to hold the cereal. Bring in a Styrofoam cup for each student. Cut a 3" square of aluminum foil and a 4" piece of string for each student.

Materials Needed

Colorful cereal O's

Small paper cups

Styrofoam cups

Pencils

Aluminum foil

String

Bows

Glue

Connections to Other Disciplines

Reading: Introduce *The Bells of Christmas* by Virginia Hamilton.

Teacher Directions

1. Put the cereal into small paper cups for the students.
2. Give each student a Styrofoam cup and a bow.
3. Hand out the rest of the materials.
4. Help students punch the two holes into the cup.

Student Directions

1. Carefully use the pencil to punch two holes into the bottom of the Styrofoam cup.

2. Think of a design to make on the cup. Then glue the pieces of cereal onto the cup to create your design. Let dry.

3. Tape a length of string onto a corner of a square of aluminum foil. Then crumple the foil into a ball, being sure to keep the string showing above it.

4. Tie the end of the string through the two holes in the cup, letting the foil ball hang down at the bottom of the bell.

5. Glue a bow to your bell to finish the project.

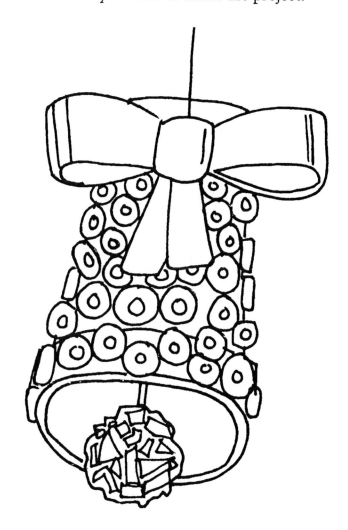

Kwanzaa

34. AFRICAN KOFI (HAT)

Grade Level: 3–4

Kwanzaa is Swahili for "the first fruit." Kwanzaa, a seven-day festival that begins on December 26, celebrates the ties between traditional African customs and African-American cultural histories. Kwanzaa focuses on seven principles: *umoja* (unity), *kujichagulia* (self-determination), *ujima* (group effort), *ujamaa* (group economics), *kuumba* (creativity), *nia* (purpose), and *imani* (faith). The *kofi* is an African hat that is worn in many traditional celebrations.

Project Description

Students will create a traditional kofi, using the geometric patterns of Africa, in celebration of Kwanzaa.

Advance Preparation

Have available one 18" square black sheet of paper for each student. Make copies of the different patterns for hats. Make an example of a finished project.

Materials Needed

Hat pattern sheets
18" square sheets of black construction paper
Craypas or chalk in red, black, and green
Scissors
Tape
Rulers

Connections to Other Disciplines

Social Studies: What is the history of Kwanzaa? Explain the festival's seven principles.

Reading: Introduce *Celebrating Kwanzaa* by Angela Shelf Medearis and *Kwanzaa: A Family Affair* by Mildred Pitts Walter.

Mathematics: Discuss geometric patterns and lines.

Teacher Directions

1. Show your example of a finished kofi.
2. Discuss the geometric designs, colors, and patterns used in the African kofi.
3. Give each student an 18" square of black paper and a kofi pattern sheet.
4. Distribute the rest of the materials.
5. Help students with measuring and folding.

Student Directions

1. On your sheet of black construction paper draw four lines, each one 6" from one edge, to form nine boxes. Fold on each line.

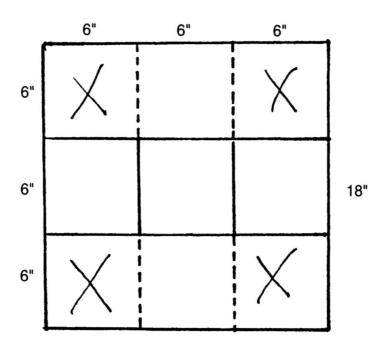

2. Open up the sheet. Decide on a geometric pattern for your kofi, and plan how you want to draw and color your design on the paper. Do *not* draw anything in the four corner boxes.

3. Now draw your design on the five remaining boxes of the paper. Be sure to use red, green, and black, the traditional Kwanzaa colors.

4. When you have finished your design, cut along the dotted lines as shown in the illustration.

5. Fold the paper into a box shape and tape the flaps in place.

6. Fold under 2" of the bottom edge inside the kofi and tape in place. (See the illustration.)

7. Proudly wear your kofi!

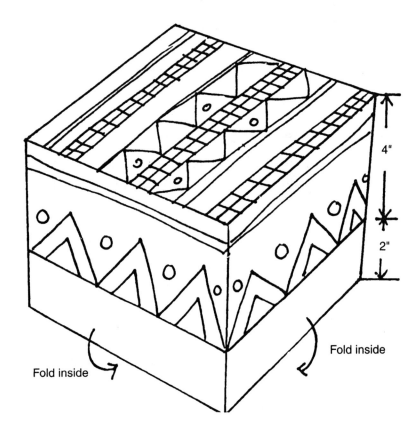

4"

2"

Fold inside

Fold inside

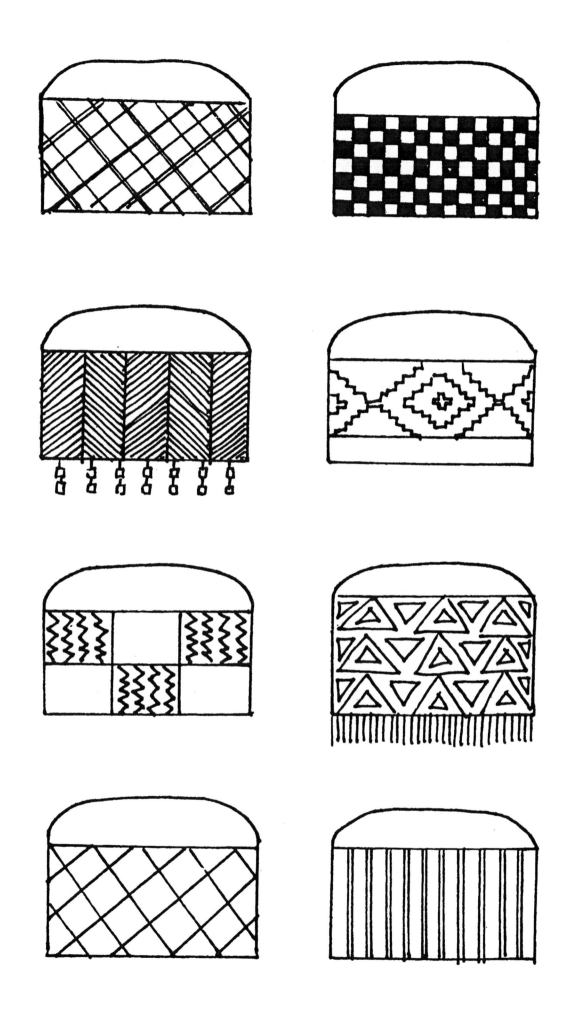

Chinese New Year

35. PAPER LANTERN

Grade Level: 2–4

The Chinese New Year is the most important holiday in China. It is a fifteen-day celebration that usually occurs in late January, ending with the festival of lanterns. The Chinese people carry paper lanterns as signposts to guide guests and spirits of ancestors to the celebration.

Project Description

Students will create a paper lantern by folding and cutting colored paper.

Advance Preparation

Make a finished sample of the paper lantern to show the students. Have enough 12" x 18" sheets of colored construction paper for each student to choose a color they like.

Materials Needed

    12" x 18" sheets of colored construction paper
    Scissors
    Stapler
    Hole punch
    String

Connections to Other Disciplines

Social Studies: Discuss the history of the Chinese New Year. Why is red such an important color in the celebration?

Mathematics: The Chinese celebrate different animals in different years. Find out what animal is celebrated for the current year. What are the animals of the years in which your students were born? How many years and animals are there all together?

Reading: Introduce *Gung Hay Fat Choy! Happy New Year* by Terry Behrens, *Chinatown* by William Low, and *Chinese New Year's Dragon* by Rachel Sing.

Cooking: Bring in Chinese sesame cookies for students to enjoy as a snack.

Teacher Directions

1. Display your completed paper lantern.
2. Let each student pick a piece of colored construction paper.
3. Hand out the rest of the materials.
4. Help students with cutting, rolling, and stapling.

Student Directions

1. Fold and crease 1" of the edge of both short ends of the colored construction paper.
2. Fold your sheet of paper in half, but do not crease it.
3. Cut 1" parallel strips across the doubled paper, stopping at the creased edges, as shown in the illustration.
4. Open up the paper. Now roll the paper (the long way) into a cylinder shape and staple together at the top and bottom.

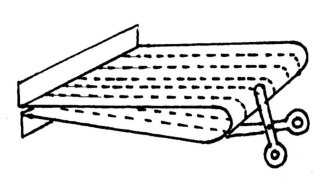

5. Punch three holes in the top strip, attach three strings as shown, and have your teacher or parent hang your lantern from a light fixture.

Optional: Crease the lantern strips to make a pattern, as shown.

36. FISH WIND SOCK

Grade Level: 3–4

The Chinese New Year celebrates animals of the zodiac. Each year is represented by one of twelve different animals. The fish is a common animal representing all of the years.

Project Description

Students will create a three-dimensional sculpture, a wind sock in the shape of a fish, to celebrate Chinese New Year. They will learn about the Chinese zodiac symbols and Japanese haiku.

Advance Preparation

Cut out fish scales by selecting two different 15" by 20" sheets of tissue paper; fold each into quarters, draw five ovals to fit the paper, then cut the scales in half (see illustration). Cut a 4" x 18" oak tag strip for each student, for the fish mouth. Complete one fish wind sock as an example. Make copies of the fin patterns.

Materials Needed

- 18" x 30" sheets of tissue paper (two sheets of different colors for each student)
- 15" x 20" sheets of tissue paper (two sheets of different colors)
- 12" x 18" oak tag (two sheets)
- Fins pattern sheets
- String
- Hole punch
- Scissors
- Glue

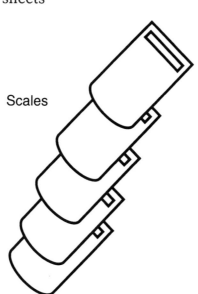

Scales

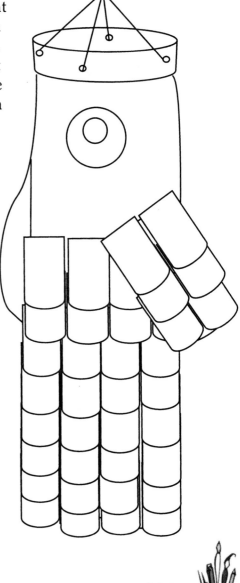

Connections to Other Disciplines

Social Studies: Discuss why fish are a major food staple in China and other Asian countries.

Reading: Explore poetry with students, including Japanese haiku. Introduce *Maples in the Mist: Children's Poems from the Tang Dynasty* by Minfong Ho, *My Chinatown: One Year in Poems* by Kam Mak, and *Red Dragonfly on My Shoulder: Haiku* translated by Sylvia Cassedy and Kunihiro Suetake.

Teacher Directions

1. Hand out two sheets of 18" x 30" different colored tissue paper to each student.
2. Hand out the pre-cut scales.
3. Show your sample assembled fish wind sock.
4. Show how to glue scales onto fish body by overlapping halved circles.
5. Hand out 4" x 18" oak tag strips for fish mouths.
6. Hand out templates of fins.

Student Directions

1. For the fish mouth, fold the 4" x 18" oak tag strip in half lengthwise, so it becomes 2" x 18".
2. For the fish body, glue the top of the two large sheets of colored tissue paper into the folded strip, then glue the folded half over the tissue at the top.
3. For the fish mouth and body, create a cylinder by overlapping the folded strip approximately 6" and gluing together.
4. Glue the side of the body together from the mouth to 12" down the body. Glue both sheets together also. Leave the remainder open for the tail.
5. Using the half circles of tissue, starting from the bottom of the body, glue the top edge of each scale, using alternating colors. Continue this pattern up to 6" from the mouth.
6. Continue making vertical rows around the body to cover the fish.
7. Create large eyes and fins using the template.
8. With the hole punch, make four holes in the mouth. Cut two sections of string, each about 24" long, and thread them through to hang the fish wind sock.

Hands-On Art Activities

SIDE
FIN

SIDE
FIN

TOP
FIN

Martin Luther King Jr. Day

37. COLOR MY WORLD

Grade Level: 3–4

This activity honors Martin Luther King Jr., the famous civil rights leader. He wanted people of all colors, races, and nationalities to live together peacefully and to respect one another.

Project Description

Students will draw their portraits and use patterns of large crayons to make frames of different skin colors.

Advance Preparation

Purchase construction paper and crayons in different skin colors. Create a crayon template out of 18" x 24" oak tag for each student. Cut 9" ovals out of white paper that will fit in the ovals on the crayon templates for each student's portrait.

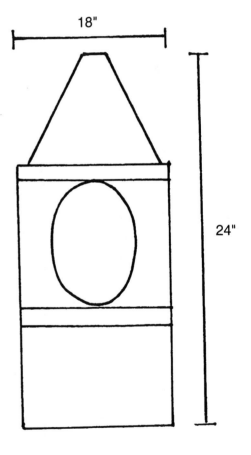

Materials Needed

- 18" x 24" colored paper in different skin shades (browns, tans, light oranges, light pinks)
- Oak tag
- White drawing paper
- Crayons in different skin shades
- Scissors
- Glue

Connections to Other Disciplines

Social Studies: What was Martin Luther King Jr.'s dream? Discuss the nationalities of the students and their dreams.

Reading: Introduce *I Have a Dream* by Martin Luther King Jr. and *Martin's Big Words: The Life of Martin Luther King Jr.* by Doreen Rappaport.

Teacher Directions

1. Give each student a crayon template and a 9" oval sheet of white paper.
2. Hand out the rest of the materials.
3. Help students with the tracing and cutting.

Student Directions

1. Select a sheet of paper that approximates your skin color.
2. Use the template to trace the crayon shape on your paper. Draw in the lines and circle as shown on the template.
3. Draw in your facial features and hair color on the white oval. Then color your face with a crayon color that approximates your skin tone.
4. Glue your finished portrait onto your large crayon pattern in the space provided.

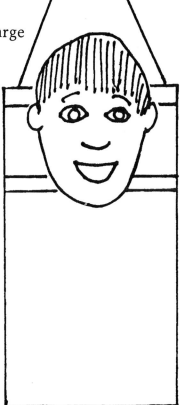

5. Display your finished crayon portrait along with your classmates' crayon portraits on a bulletin board.

Think of a title for your bulletin board display, such as "We Bring Color to Your Life," "Color Our World," "Let's Celebrate Colors." Take a class vote to decide on the final title.

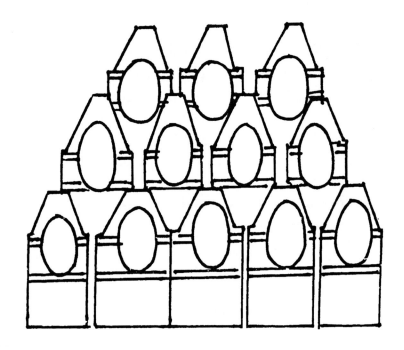

Groundhog Day

38. GROUNDHOG PUPPET

Grade Level: K–2
February 2 is Groundhog Day. According to legend, if the groundhog sees its shadow, we will have six more weeks of cold weather!

Project Description
Students will create a groundhog puppet.

Advance Preparation
Make a copy of the groundhog pattern and have two sheets of 9" x 12" brown construction paper for each student. Prepare one 1" x 12" cardboard strip for each student.

Materials Needed
    9" x 12" sheets of brown construction paper
    Groundhog pattern sheets
    Cardboard
    Glue
    Scissors
    Crayons
    Stapler

Connections to Other Disciplines
Science: Discuss the cycle of seasons, which occurs because of the sun's position.

Social Studies: Discuss the history of groundhogs (or woodchucks) and their importance to Native Americans.

Reading: Introduce *Wake up, Groundhog!* by Carol L. Cohen.

Teacher Directions

1. Give each student two sheets of 9" x 12" brown construction paper, a groundhog pattern, and an oak tag strip.
2. Distribute the rest of the materials.
3. Help students staple and assemble.

Student Directions

1. Place the two pieces of brown paper together and staple along the two outer sides.
2. Cut a wavy line along the top of both pieces.
3. Color in your groundhog pattern and cut it out.
4. Glue your groundhog to the cardboard strip, leaving enough of the strip showing as a handle for you to hold.
5. Place your groundhog between the two pieces of brown paper. You can now move your groundhog up and down.
6. Stand near a window with the groundhog and see if the groundhog makes a shadow. Will there be six more weeks of winter?

Valentine's Day

39. VALENTINE MOBILE

Grade Level: 1–3
Valentine's Day is a special time to remember our friends and families with words and gifts that show we care about them.

Project Description
Students will create a heart mobile.

Advance Preparation
Cut different colors of construction paper into 3" squares. Purchase cotton balls.

Materials Needed
   Oak tag
   Hole punch
   Glue
   Cotton balls
   Colored construction paper
   Pencils
   Scissors
   String

Connections to Other Disciplines
Science: Explore cloud formations and the different kinds of clouds (cirrus, cumulus, stratus, nimbostratus, and so on).

Reading: Introduce *Cloudy with a Chance of Meatballs* by Judi Barrett, *The Cloud Book* by Tomie dePaola, and *Hi, Clouds* by Carol Greene.

Teacher Directions
   1. Give each student a sheet of oak tag, some cotton balls, and several squares of colored construction paper.
   2. Distribute the rest of the materials.
   3. Help students as needed.

Student Directions

1. Draw a cloud shape about 8" wide on the oak tag.
2. Punch several holes in the bottom of the cloud and one hole in the center of the top of the cloud.

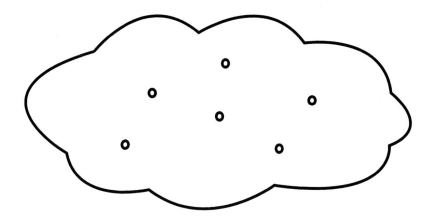

3. Glue cotton balls onto the cloud. Let dry.
4. Fold the paper squares in half, draw half heart shapes along the folds, and cut out the hearts.
5. Punch out a hole at the top of each heart.
6. Tie a different length of string to each heart.
7. Write a different valentine message on each heart.
8. Tie each heart to the cloud.
9. Tie a string to the top of the cloud to display your mobile.

40. 3D VALENTINE'S DAY CARD

Grade Level: 1–5

According to one legend, Valentine's Day originated in third-century Rome to honor Valentinus, a Catholic bishop. Soldiers at the time were banned from being married because they were needed to fight in the wars. Valentinus secretly performed marriage ceremonies for those soldiers; when this was discovered, he was imprisoned. While in prison, Valentinus befriended the jailer's blind young daughter, whom he is said to have miraculously healed before his death. He left a farewell message to her, "From your Valentine."

Project Description

Students will create a three-dimensional valentine card.

Advance Preparation

Obtain metallic paper and cellophane.

Materials Needed

8-1/2" x 11" sheet of white paper for each student

Metallic paper (or construction paper)

Cellophane in red or pink

Markers

Scissors

Glue

Connections to Other Disciplines

Language Arts: Explore the language used on valentine cards. Is the language sometimes "flowery"? Are poems and limericks used?

Reading: Introduce *Roses Are Pink, Your Feet Really Stink* by Diane De Groat.

Teacher Directions

1. Give each student an 8-1/2" x 11" sheet of white paper.

2. Distribute the rest of the materials

3. Help students as needed.

114

Student Directions

1. Fold the white paper in half.

2. Fold the front cover in half again and draw a half heart along the fold. (See the illustration.)

3. Cut out the heart.

4. Cut out small hearts from the metallic paper.

5. Glue these metallic hearts to the inside of the card. Create any collage design you'd like.

6. Cut a rectangle from the cellophane paper that's a bit bigger than the cutout heart on the card.

7. Glue the cellophane to the inside of the front cover.

8. Write your Valentine's Day greeting on the front of the card.

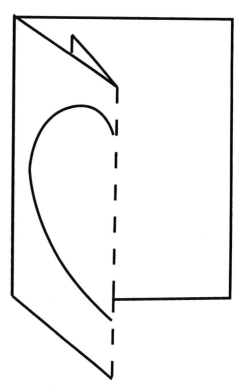

41. CONCENTRIC HEARTS

Grade Level: 2–4
Give a homemade heart card to someone you love.

Project Description
Students will create a heart card using concentric heart patterns.

Advance Preparation
Purchase enough white construction paper in the sizes needed to give each student one piece of each size. Have a 14" x 18" sheet of oak tag for each student.

Materials Needed
12" x 14", 14" x 16", and 16" x 18" sheets of white construction paper

14" x 18" sheets of white oak tag

Scissors

Glue

Craypas

Black markers

Connections to Other Disciplines

Language Arts: Discuss the relationship between poetry and Valentine's Day.

Cooking: Prepare layered heart cookies using heart cookie cutters of various sizes. Layer the graduated size heart-shaped cookie dough cutouts one atop the other, from large to small.

Reading: Introduce *Roses Are Pink, Your Feet Really Stink* by Diane De Groat and *Poetry by Heart: A Child's Book of Poems to Remember* edited by Liz Attenborough.

Teacher Directions
1. Give each student one piece of each size of white construction paper and one sheet of oak tag.
2. Hand out the rest of the materials.
3. Help students with cutting and gluing.

Student Directions

1. Cut out different sized hearts from the three different sizes of white construction paper.
2. Glue the largest heart to the white oak tag. Let dry.
3. Glue the middle-sized heart on top of the largest heart. Let dry.
4. Glue the smallest heart on top of the middle-sized heart. Let dry.
5. Use a different color of craypas to color the portions of each heart showing.
6. Use a black marker to write a Valentine message on the smallest heart.

42. VALENTINE QUILT

Grade Level: 2–4

Quilts, which are made of patches of different fabrics, have been popular in America since the eighteenth century. Heart shapes were often used in quilt patterns, particularly by the Pennsylvania Dutch.

Project Description

Students will create a class quilt of heart patterns.

Advance Preparation

Get a 2' x 3' piece of patterned material to use as the background for the quilt. Cut enough 4" squares of patterned material to make a heart for each student. Prepare a 2" x 3" heart template out of oak tag for each student. Cut 5" squares of felt in different colors.

Materials Needed

2' x 3' piece of patterned material

Oak tag

4" squares of patterned material

5" squares of felt

White glue

Connections to Other Disciplines

Social Studies: Discuss the importance of quilts in U.S. history. What is a "quilting bee"?

Reading: Introduce *The Patchwork Quilt* by Valerie Flournay, *The Quilt Story* by Tony Johnston, and *The Quilt* by Ann Jonas.

Teacher Directions

1. Hang the 2' x 3' piece of material on a wall.
2. Give each student a 4" square of patterned fabric, an oak tag heart template, and a 5" square of felt.
3. Hand out the rest of the materials.
4. Help students with cutting and gluing.

Student Directions

1. Use the heart template to trace a heart on a piece of patterned material.

2. Cut out the heart and glue it to a piece of felt.

3. Look at the large piece of material your teacher has prepared and hung on the wall. Decide where you would like to put your cutout heart, and glue it in that spot on the material.

4. When your classmates have all done the same and are finished, stand back and enjoy looking at the Valentine quilt.

43. FLOWERY HEART

Grade Level: 3–4

This flowery heart looks like the cover of an old-fashioned valentine candy box.

Project Description

Students will create a three-dimensional heart with floral designs.

Advance Preparation

Make a sample heart to display. Buy enough sheets of 8-1/2" x 11" red construction paper and 12" x 18" sheets of white construction paper to give one to each student. Have other colors of construction paper, including green and white, available for the flowers.

Materials Needed

8-1/2" x 11" sheets of red construction paper

12" x 18" sheets of white construction paper

Construction paper in variety of colors

Scissors

Glue

Markers

Connections to Other Disciplines

Science: Talk about the human heart and what we can do to take care of it (eat healthy foods, exercise).

Reading: Introduce *Valentine's Day: Story and Pictures* by Miriam Nerlove.

Teacher Directions

1. Display your sample valentine heart.
2. Give each student one sheet of 8-1/2" x 11" red construction paper and one sheet of 12" x 18" white construction paper.
3. Help students with cutting and gluing.

Student Directions

1. Cut a heart out of the red paper by folding the paper in half and cutting as shown by your teacher.

2. Glue the red heart to the white construction paper. Let dry.
3. Draw a scalloped edge around the red heart and cut it out.
4. Cut out flower petals in a variety of colors.
5. Cut green leaves and stems, and white circles for flower centers.
6. Glue the circle centers, the leaves and stems, and the petals onto the heart. Let dry.
7. Fold up each petal so that the petals bend away from the paper background.

Who will you give your Valentine heart to?

St. Patrick's Day

44. POT O' GOLD RAINBOW

Grade Level: 1–3

St. Patrick's Day honors the patron saint of Ireland. On St. Patrick's Day, people wear lots of green and put up decorations of four-leafed clover and leprechauns. According to an Irish legend, leprechauns hide pots of gold at the end of a rainbow.

Project Description

Students will create a drawing of a rainbow with a pot of gold.

Advance Preparation

Cut gold wrapping paper and black construction paper into 6" squares for each student. Have a 12" x 18" sheet of white drawing paper for each student.

Materials Needed

Crayons

12" x 18" sheets of white drawing paper

Black construction paper

White chalk

Scissors

Glue

Gold wrapping paper

Tape

Connections to Other Disciplines

Science: Discuss how rainbows are formed. Ask if any students have seen a rainbow in the sky. Also discuss the spectrum of colors seen in a rainbow.

Social Studies: Discuss some of the legends of Ireland and stories of saints, such as Saint Patrick.

Language Arts: Help students write stories about leprechauns and their pots of gold.

Mathematics: Describe arcs.

Reading: Introduce *St. Patrick's Day* by Elizabeth O'Donnell.

Teacher Directions

1. Give each student a sheet of 12" x 18" white drawing paper, a 6" square of black construction paper, and a 6" square of gold wrapping paper.
2. Distribute the rest of the materials.
3. Help students with drawing the arcs, cutting, and gluing.

Student Directions

1. Draw five or six arcs on your white paper to make a rainbow.
2. Draw a cloud at each end of the rainbow.
3. Color each arc a different color.
4. Color the sky blue.
5. Fold the black paper in half, use white chalk to draw half of a pot, and then cut out the pot.
6. Open out the pot. Use white chalk to color in a small area on the pot for a shiny spot.
7. Glue the black pot under the rainbow, between the two clouds.
8. Cut out six or seven circles from the gold paper and glue them above the pot under the rainbow.
9. Tape your "pot o' gold" rainbow picture to a window.

Spring and Summer

General

45. FLOWER PIÑATA

Grade Level: 2–4

A piñata is a papier-mâché figure that traditionally is filled with trinkets and candies. A person who is blindfolded tries to hit and break open the hanging piñata with a stick so that the contents fall out. No one is sure where the piñata originated. Objects similar to modern piñatas were used by the Chinese, Europeans, Africans, and Native South Americans. But these days, piñatas are usually associated with Mexico. These piñatas will be for show to celebrate cultural freedom.

Project Description

Students will create a piñata using a paper bag and tissue paper.

Advance Preparation

Obtain a brown lunch bag for each group of four students. Have a large supply of packing "peanuts." Buy colored tissue paper and ribbon.

Materials Needed

Brown paper lunch bags

Colored tissue paper

Crayons or marker

Scissors

Glue

Packing peanuts

Stapler

Ribbon

String

Connections to Other Disciplines

Social Studies: Discuss the history of the piñata and how it has been used in different cultures.

Reading: Introduce *El Piñata, the Piñata Maker* by George Ancona.

Teacher Directions

1. Divide the class into groups of four students.
2. Give each group a lunch bag and a supply of packing peanuts.
3. Hand out the rest of the materials.
4. Help students with cutting and assembling.

Student Directions

1. You and your group will work together to create a piñata. Begin by cutting tissue paper into strips. Then cut fringe in the strips, leaving a 1" edge at the top (see the illustration).

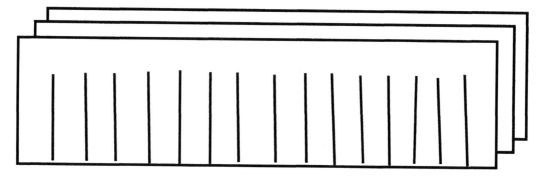

2. Glue the fringed strips of tissue paper to the lunch bag, beginning at the bottom of the bag and working up to the top opening. Glue the strips only at the top and in layers so that the fringe is loose.
3. Draw flower shapes on the white construction paper.
4. Color the flower shapes and cut them out.
5. Glue the flowers to the overlapping fringes on the bag.
6. Stuff the bag with the packing peanuts and staple the bag closed.
7. Finish the piñata with a ribbon bow and tie string at the top.
8. Hang your group's piñata.

46. FLOWER WALL HANGING

Grade Level: 2–5
Colorful flowers are a welcome sight in the sunny, warm days of spring!

Project Description
Students will create a flower wall hanging with an accompanying poem or story.

Advance Preparation
Cut sheets of tissue paper of different colors into 2" squares. Have writing paper and plenty of 18" x 24" sheets of colored construction paper.

Materials Needed
18" x 24" sheets of colored construction paper

Colored tissue paper

Markers

Writing paper

Scissors

Glue

Connections to Other Disciplines

Language Arts: Explore the various types of writing styles—expository, poetry, narration, play, and so on.

Science: Discuss the kinds of flowers found in your neighborhood. Do they flower once each year? Are they in bloom for several weeks?

Reading: Introduce *A Seed, a Flower, a Minute, an Hour* by Joan W. Blos.

Teacher Directions
1. Give each student three sheets of 18" x 24" colored construction paper.
2. Distribute the rest of the materials.
3. Help students with their poems or stories as needed.

Student Directions

1. Draw a large flower shape on one sheet of colored construction paper.

24"

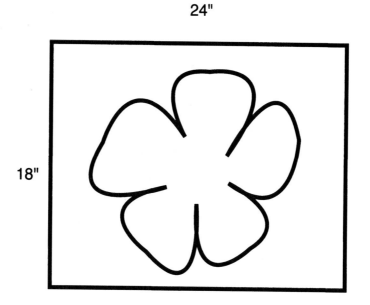

18"

2. Draw a smaller flower shape on a half sheet of colored construction paper.

3. Cut out both flowers.

4. Glue the smaller flower on top of the larger flower only in the center. Let dry.

5. Roll the tissue paper squares into small balls and glue them to the center of the flower (see the final illustration).

9"

12"

6. Gently pull up the edges of the two flowers so that they stand up a bit.

7. Glue the finished flower at the bottom of the third sheet of paper.

8. Write a poem or a few sentences about flowers. Use the writing paper and markers.

9. When finished, glue your writing paper to the flower sheet above the flower.

10. Display your flower wall hanging.

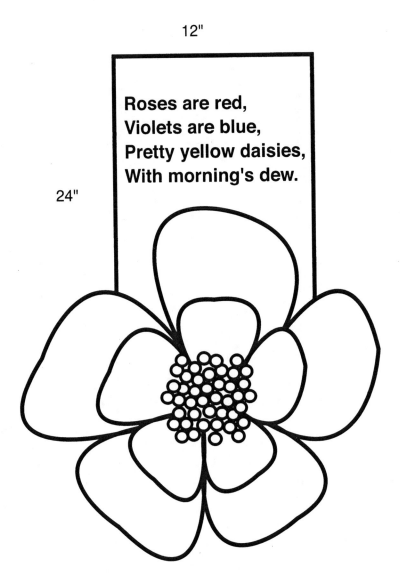

12"

24"

Roses are red,
Violets are blue,
Pretty yellow daisies,
With morning's dew.

130

47. "GONE FISHING"

Grade Level: 1–2

This three-dimensional sculpture shows a hobby many kids enjoy in the spring and summer.

Project Description

Students will create a sculpture of a child fishing.

Advance Preparation

Make one copy of the "Gone Fishing" pattern sheet for each student. Obtain oak tag, small white paper cups, and straws. Cut one 8" length of yarn for each student.

Materials Needed

"Gone Fishing" pattern sheets

Markers

Oak tag

Small white paper cups

Straws

Yarn

Stapler

Glue

Connections to Other Disciplines

Language Arts: Discuss what students like to do in their free time. Do they have hobbies? Play sports?

Science: Discuss where fish live (oceans, rivers, lakes, streams, ponds). Show pictures of different kinds of fish.

Reading: Introduce *What's It Like to Be a Fish?* by Wendy Pfeffer and *Rosie's Fishing Trip* by Amy Hest.

Teacher Directions

1. Give each student one "Gone Fishing" pattern sheet, one piece of oak tag, one paper cup, one straw, and one 8" piece of yarn.
2. Hand out the rest of the materials.
3. Help students with tracing, cutting, and stapling.

Student Directions

1. Cut the pieces out of the pattern sheet.
2. Trace the patterns onto oak tag and cut out each piece.
3. Color the pieces.
4. Your teacher will help you staple the arms to the paper cup and the hands to the straw.
5. Decide if your fisherman will be a girl or a boy. Then fold the head at the fold line and glue the head to the cup's bottom.
6. Fold the two legs at the fold lines and glue the legs to the inside of the cup.
7. Glue the yarn to the end of the straw, and glue the fish to the other end of the yarn.
8. Seat your fisher girl or fisher boy on the edge of a table.

Hands-On Art Activities

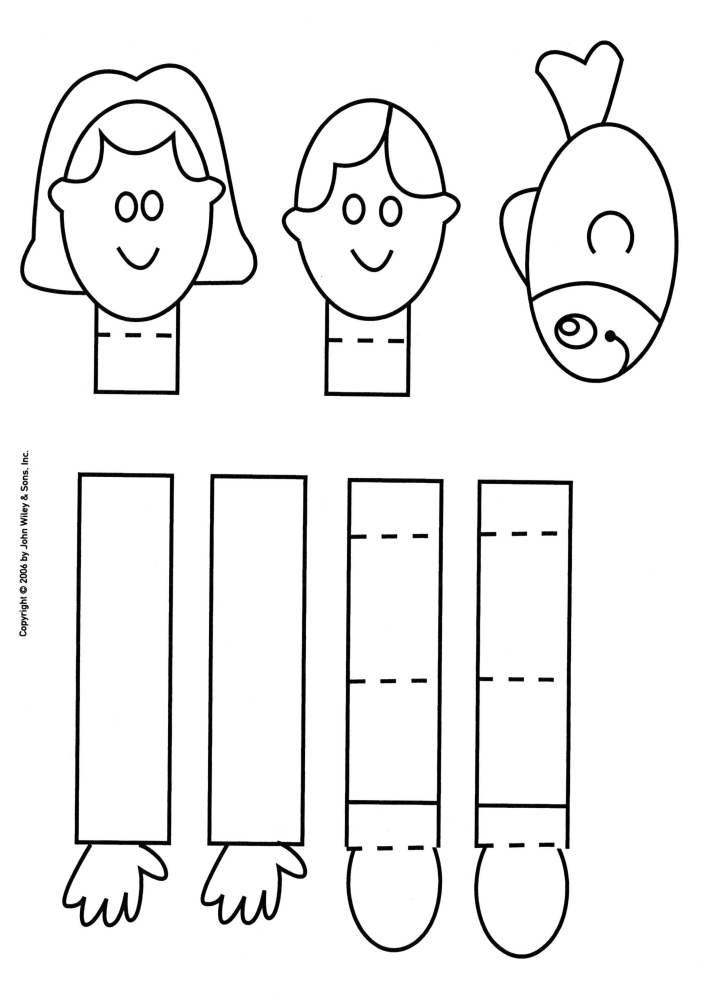

48. FROG AND LILY PAD MURAL

Grade Level: K–2
This mural makes a great display for a spring bulletin board.

Project Description
Students will create a mural of frogs on lily pads.

Advance Preparation
Make one copy of each of the pattern sheets for each student. Obtain 3' x 6' mural paper and 1" yellow pom-poms (one for each student). Paint the water and some plants and rocks around the edges of the mural to suggest a pond.

Materials Needed
3' x 6' mural paper
Flower pattern sheets
Lily pad and frog pattern sheets
Crayons
Scissors
Glue
1" yellow pom-poms

Connections to Other Disciplines
Science: Talk about frogs and show pictures of different kinds. Explain that a frog lives mostly in the water and a toad lives mostly on land. What other animals might live in a pond?

Reading: Introduce the *Frog and Toad* series by Arnold Lobel, *At the Frog Pond* by Tilde Michels, and *Turtle, Turtle, Watch Out!* by April Pulley Sayre.

Teacher Directions
1. Give each student one copy of the flower pattern sheet and one copy of the lily pad and frog pattern sheet.
2. Distribute the rest of the materials.
3. Help students with cutting and gluing.

134

Student Directions

1. Cut out the three flowers. Leave them white. Set aside.
2. Color the lily pad green.
3. Color the frog any color you want.
4. Cut out the lily pad and the frog.
5. Spread a little glue on the lily pad where shown and press the largest white flower to that spot.
6. Put a little bit of glue on the largest white flower where shown and press the middle-sized white flower to that spot.
7. Spread a little bit of glue on the middle-sized white flower where shown and press the smallest white flower to that spot.
8. Glue a yellow pom-pom to the center of the smallest white flower.
9. Glue the frog wherever you would like on the lily pad.
10. Your teacher will help you glue your lily pad to the pond mural.
11. As a finishing touch, gently pull up the petals on the three white flowers to make them stand up a bit.

Glue

Glue

Glue

Earth Day

49. WORLD MOBILE

Grade Level: 3–5

Earth Day began in 1970 as a way to get people to focus on the natural wonders of our planet and to think about how to protect our environment.

Project Description

Students will create a mobile for Earth Day.

Advance Preparation

Make a copy of the world map patterns for each student. Cut oak tag circles that are the same size as the pattern pieces (four for each student). Bring in index cards (you will need four for each student) and string.

Materials Needed

World map pattern sheets

Oak tag

Scissors

Index cards

String

Hole punch

Markers

Glue

Connections to Other Disciplines

Science: Discuss preservation of natural resources. What can students do to help preserve the natural areas (rainforest, rivers, mountains, and so on) on Earth?

Social Studies: Talk about Earth Day and introduce students to several people who have tried to help protect the environment and wildlife, such as Rachel Carson and Jane Goodall.

Reading: Introduce *Ecology* by Steve Pollock and *Prentice Hall Science Explorer: Environmental Science* by Michael J. Padilla, Ioannis Miaoulis, and Martha Cyr.

138

Teacher Directions

1. Give each student four oak tag circles, four index cards, and one set of world map patterns (total of four maps).
2. Distribute the rest of the materials.
3. Help students with cutting, gluing, and punching holes.

Student Directions

1. Cut out the four world maps from the pattern sheets.
2. Glue each map to a different oak tag circle. Let dry.
3. Take one pair of the maps and glue them together back to back. Let dry.
4. Take the remaining pair of maps and glue these together back to back. Let dry.
5. Cut along the dotted line on the globes, stopping where the dotted line ends.
6. Insert the two globes together so they fit to form an X.
7. On your four index cards, write something about the Earth, such as a fact about geography or about an animal or plant. The choice is yours.

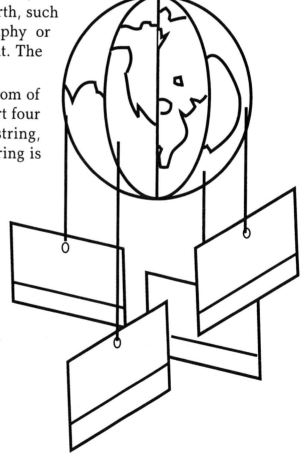

8. Punch a hole at the bottom of each globe section, insert four different lengths of string, and tie a knot so the string is secured to the globe.
9. Punch a hole at the top of each of your completed index cards, run the string through it, and tie a knot to secure it.
10. Display your Earth Day mobile in the classroom.

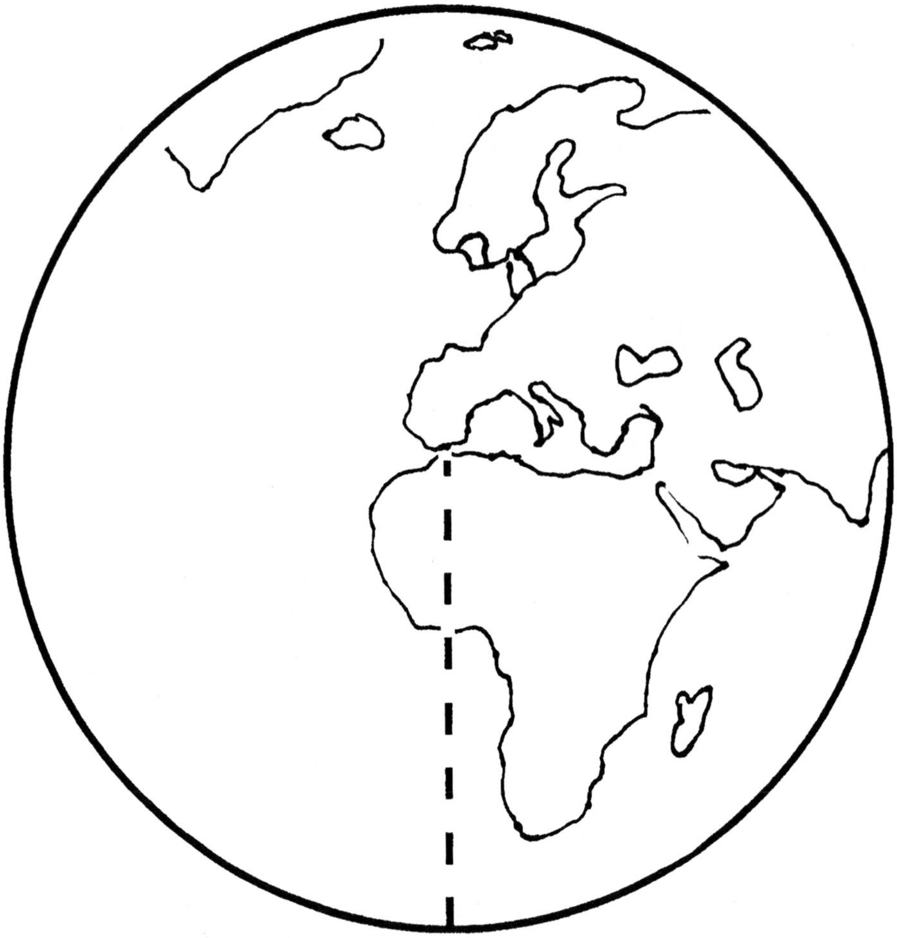

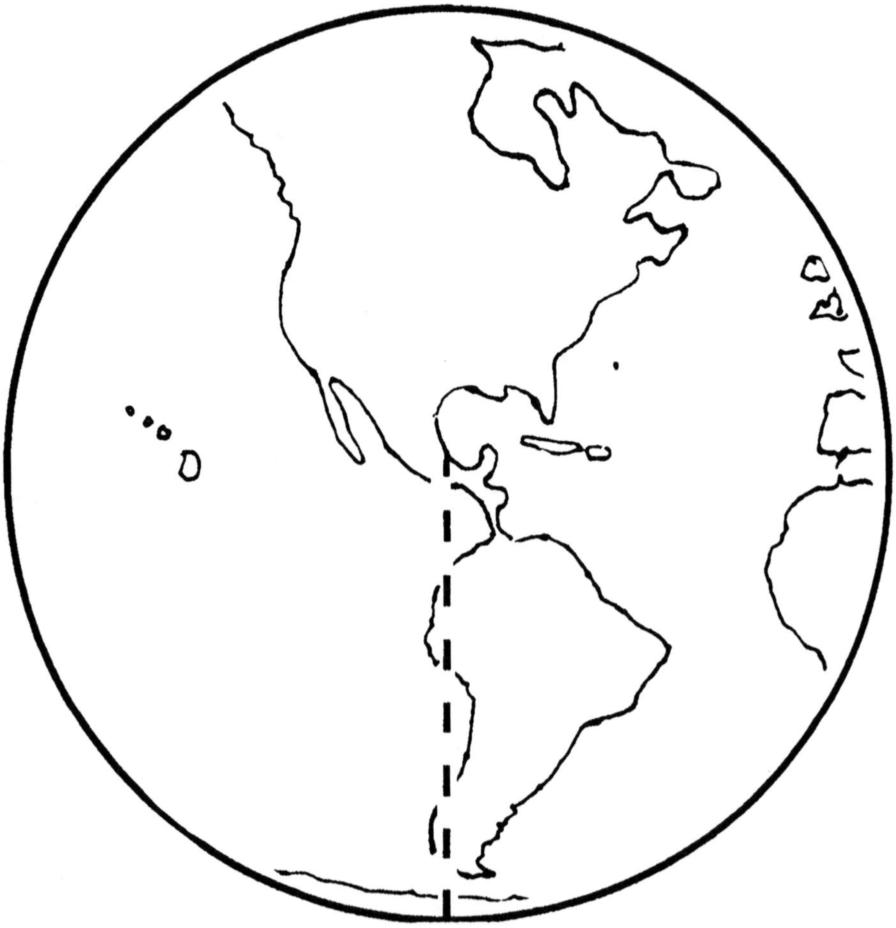

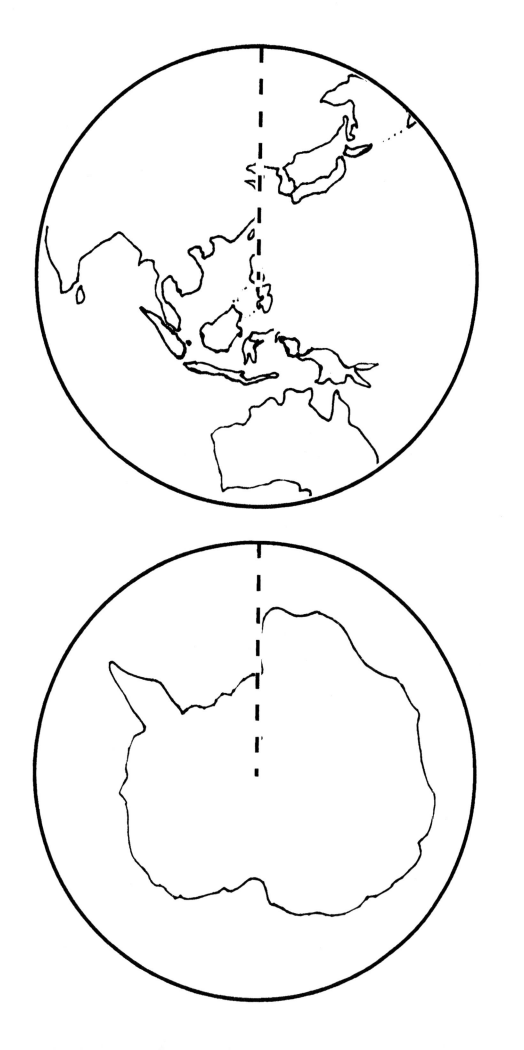

Passover

50. SEDER PLACE SETTING

Grade Level: 2–3

The seder is a feast traditionally served on Passover, a Jewish holiday celebrating the exodus of the Israelites from Egypt, where they had been kept in slavery. Traditional foods served at the seder dinner symbolize this time in Jewish history. Bitter herbs, such as horseradish, symbolize the bitterness of slavery; *charoses,* a mixture of fruits and nuts with wine, symbolizes the mortar made by the slaves; matzos (unleavened bread) symbolize the haste of departure from Egypt; roasted shankbone symbolizes the sacrificial lamb offered at the temple; roasted egg symbolizes another offering; *karpas* (a green vegetable such as parsley) symbolizes a time of new life in the spring; and salt water symbolizes the sweat and tears of the slaves.

Project Description

Students will create a seder place setting.

Advance Preparation

Bring in Styrofoam cups, plastic utensils, napkins, and paper plates. Obtain or create your own pictures of the special foods served at a seder.

Materials Needed

12" x 18" sheets of white paper

Styrofoam cups

Plastic forks, knives, and spoons

Paper napkins

White paper plates

Markers

Scissors

Glue

Connections to Other Disciplines

Social Studies: Discuss the history of Passover. Talk about the various foods that are eaten by different people around the world during their special celebrations.

142

Reading: Introduce *Jewish Holidays All Year Around: A Family Treasury* by Mir Tamim Ansary, *Matzo Ball Moon* by Leslea Newman, and *Table Manners* by Vladimir Radunsky and Chris Raschka.

Teacher Directions

1. Discuss the Passover seder and display pictures of the special foods served at a seder.
2. Cut the Styrofoam cups in half so that each student has a half cup.
3. Give each student a 12" x 18" sheet of white paper.
4. Distribute the rest of the materials.

Student Directions

1. Place the white paper in front of you so that the long side is at the top.
2. Decorate the paper for a placemat. Set aside.
3. Draw six circles on the white paper plate, as shown in the diagram.
4. In each circle, draw one of the special types of food served at a seder.
5. Use markers to decorate your half cup.
6. Glue each piece of the place setting onto your decorated placemat.

51. MOSAIC CUP

Grade Level: 2–4

For the Passover seder, a special cup called a *kiddush* cup is put on the table. Ceremonial wine is drunk from the kiddush cup four times during the meal.

Project Description

Students will create a mosaic cup.

Advance Preparation

Find examples of mosaics in tile floors, artwork, and so on. Bring in one clear plastic cup for each student. Prepare small containers to hold one part water and one part glue.

Materials Needed

Clear plastic cups

Cellophane or colored tissue paper in various colors

White glue

Scissors

Paintbrushes

Connections to Other Disciplines

Mathematics: Discuss and display different shapes and patterns.

Reading: Introduce *On Passover* by Cathy Fishman, *The First Passover* by Leslie Swartz, and *Building with Paper* by E. Richard Churchill.

Teacher Directions

1. Explain that a cup is used at the traditional dinner called a seder at Passover.
2. Display the various examples of mosaics that you have collected.
3. Give each student one plastic cup and pass out the rest of the materials.

Student Directions

1. Cut out 1" squares from the colored paper.
2. Use a paintbrush and a small amount of the glue mixture to attach the squares to the plastic cup. You can use either a random mosaic design or a pattern.
3. Let the glue dry.

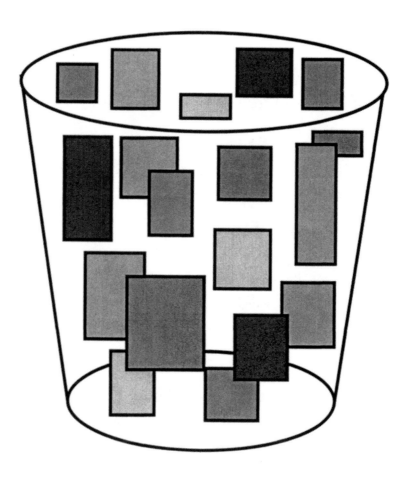

Easter

52. BUNNY BOOKMARK

Grade Level: K–2
This Easter Bunny helps students mark their place in books they are reading.

Project Description

Students will create a bunny bookmark.

Advance Preparation

Make copies of the bunny patterns, and cut apart the patterns so that each child will have one bunny box. Provide one craft stick for each student.

Materials Needed

Bunny pattern sheets

Craft sticks

Markers or crayons

Scissors

Glue

Connections to Other Disciplines

Science: Discuss the various kinds of rabbits that are found in the wild (snowshoe hares, jack rabbit, and so on).

Reading: Introduce *Rabbit's Morning* by Nancy Tafuri, *Rabbit Garden* by Miska Miles, and *The Bunny Who Found Easter* by Charlotte Zolotow. Be sure students have their bunny bookmarks nearby!

146

Teacher Directions

1. Give each student one bunny pattern and a craft stick.
2. Hand out the rest of the materials.
3. Help students with cutting and gluing.

Student Directions

1. Cut out the bunny.
2. Color your bunny and decorate the craft stick.
3. Glue the bunny to the top end of the stick.
4. Use your bunny bookmark with your next book!

53. PEEK-A-BOO CHICK

Grade Level: 1–3
Have the class make up a story using their finished Easter chicks.

Project Description
Students will create a three-dimensional pop-up chick puppet.

Advance Preparation
Each student will need two wiggly eyes, one yellow pom-pom, one small paper cup, and one unsharpened pencil. Make a hole in the bottom center of each cup. Make a sample project to show the students.

Materials Needed
    1" squares of orange construction paper

    Wiggly eyes

    Yellow pom-poms

    Unsharpened pencils

    Small paper cups

    White glue

Connections to Other Disciplines
Language Arts: Encourage students to tell stories using their peek-a-boo chicks.

Teacher Directions
1. Display your finished project and show how the chick moves up and down.
2. Give each student one 1" square of orange construction paper, two wiggly eyes, one yellow pom-pom, one unsharpened pencil, and one small paper cup with a hole in the bottom.
3. Distribute the rest of the materials.
4. Help students with the construction.

Student Directions

1. Fold the orange construction paper in half to form a triangle. This will be the chick's beak.

2. Glue the wiggly eyes to the yellow pom-pom, and glue the beak below the eyes.

3. Glue the chick to the top part of a pencil. Let dry.

4. Insert the pencil through the hole at the bottom of the cup. Your peek-a-boo chick can now move up and down!

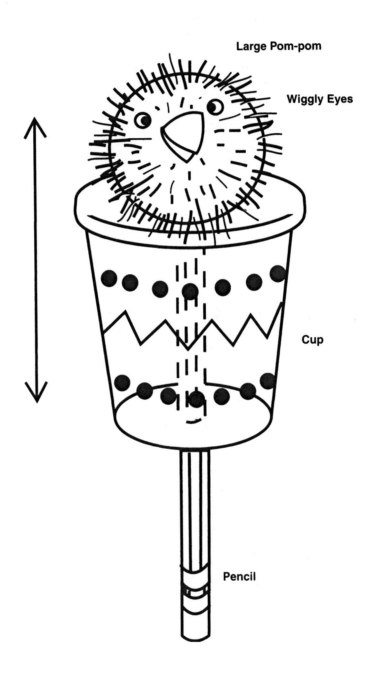

Large Pom-pom

Wiggly Eyes

Cup

Pencil

Hands-On Art Activities

54. PAPER BASKET

Grade Level: 2–3

Baskets are a traditional part of Easter. Children in Germany and Switzerland make nests of grass in the garden for the Easter Bunny to fill with eggs. Perhaps that's why we have the custom of putting green (or purple, yellow, or pink) "grass" in Easter baskets.

Project Description

Students will create a paper woven basket with colored eggs and a bunny.

Advance Preparation

Make copies of the basket pattern and the eggs, bunny, and bow pattern sheet. Cut different colored construction paper into 1/2" x 8" strips.

Materials Needed

Basket pattern sheets

Eggs, bunny, bow pattern sheets

Colored construction paper

Scissors

Crayons

Glue

Connections to Other Disciplines

Social Studies: Explore the importance of basket making and weaving to people of different cultures, such as Native American and African.

Reading: Introduce *The Big Bunny and the Easter Eggs* by Steven Kroll.

Teacher Directions

1. Give each student one basket pattern sheet and one eggs, bunny, and bow pattern sheet.
2. Distribute the rest of the materials.
3. Show students how to weave the paper strips into the basket, using the "under and over" method.
4. Help students as needed with the cutting and gluing.

Student Directions

1. Cut out the basket.
2. Carefully cut along the six horizontal lines.
3. Weave several strips of paper into the basket. Your teacher can help you.
4. Color the pictures of the eggs, bunny, and bow.
5. Cut out the eggs, bunny, and bow.
6. Glue these pictures onto your finished basket.

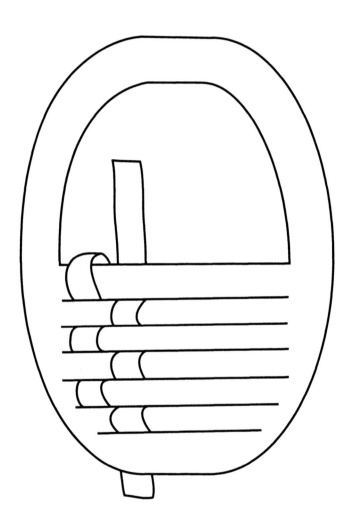

Hands-On Art Activities

Cinco de Mayo

55. CINCO DE MAYO SOMBRERO

Grade Level: 1–4

Cinco de Mayo (May 5) is a Mexican holiday celebrating the country's victory over the French at the Battle of Puebla in 1862. The sombrero is a traditional Mexican hat.

Project Description

Students will create a Mexican sombrero.

Advance Preparation

Get a box of O-shaped cereal and place ten pieces in a small cup for each student. Provide 12" x 18" sheets of white or tan construction paper. Cut a 2" x 18" strip of construction paper for each student. Make a sample sombrero.

Materials Needed

Box of O-shaped cereal

Small cups

12" x 18" sheets of white or tan construction paper

Crayons or markers

Scissors

String

Hole punch

Tape

Connections to Other Disciplines

Social Studies: Discuss the history of Cinco de Mayo (May 5).

Music: Teach students the Mexican Hat Dance.

Reading: Introduce *Uncle Nacho's Hat* by Harriet Rohmer, *Fiesta U.S.A.* by George Ancona, and *Mexican Independence Day and Cinco de Mayo* by Dianne M. Macmillan. Encourage students to wear their sombreros during reading sessions.

Teacher Directions

1. Show your sample sombrero to the class.
2. Give each student a small cup holding about ten pieces of O-shaped cereal and two 12" x 18" sheets of construction paper. (Tell students not to eat the cereal!)
3. Hand out the rest of the materials.
4. Have students follow along as you draw the sombrero outline on the chalkboard.
5. Help students with cutting and assembling.
6. Help students attach the front and back of their sombreros.

Student Directions

1. Place the construction paper in front of you and follow along as your teacher draws the sombrero outline on the chalkboard. Do your best to draw the sombrero on your paper. You need two sombreros: a front and a back.
2. Color your sombrero.
3. Cut out the two sombrero shapes.
4. Punch ten holes along the edge of the sombrero's brim.
5. To make a decorative fringe for your sombrero, tie a small length of string to each cereal piece. Insert a string through each hole and tie it off each string.

6. Your teacher will help you attach the front and back together with tape.

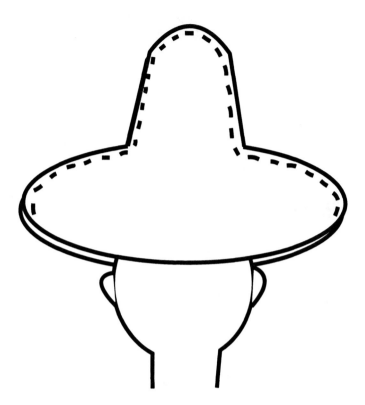

Mother's Day

56. TEAPOT TEA BAG HOLDER

Grade Level: 1–3

Mother's Day, which is celebrated on the second Sunday in May, honors all mothers for their kindness, caring, giving, love, tenderness, and intelligence.

Project Description

Students will create a tea bag holder for Mother's Day. (*Note:* Be sensitive to individual student's family situations.)

Advance Preparation

Make one copy of the teapot pattern sheet. Bring in two tea bags for each student.

Materials Needed

Teapot pattern sheets

Tea bags

Crayons

Scissors

Stapler

Connections to Other Disciplines

Science: Discuss how tea is grown and the regions that grow it. Explain that tea can be bought in bags or loose. Show samples of different varieties.

Social Studies: Discuss the different traditions of serving tea in places like England, India, and Japan.

Music: Teach younger students "I'm a Little Teapot" and the accompanying movements.

Teacher Directions

1. Give each student a copy of the teapot pattern.
2. Distribute the rest of the materials.
3. Help students with cutting and stapling.

Student Directions

1. Color and decorate your teapot.
2. Cut out the teapot pattern.
3. Fold on the dotted line.
4. Carefully staple along the edge as shown so that the teapot has an opening at the top.
5. Put the two tea bags inside the teapot.

Mother's Day Teapot

Flag Day

57. "HANDS ACROSS AMERICA" FLAG

Grade Level: K–5

For more than two hundred years the American flag has been a symbol of our nation's strength and unity. Celebrate Flag Day on June 14 by making a flag with linked hands.

Project Description

Students will create a mural to celebrate Flag Day.

Advance Preparation

Prepare a flag on a bulletin board or wall using 3' x 6' white paper. Divide the paper into the flag components and color the field blue with white stars. Have enough red construction paper to give each student one sheet. Provide black markers.

Materials Needed

3' x 6' sheet of white paper

Red construction paper

Scissors

Black markers

Glue

Connections to Other Disciplines

Social Studies: Discuss the history of the U.S. flag. Show how the flag has changed through the years.

Reading: Introduce *Red, White, and Blue: The Story of the American Flag* by John Herman.

Teacher Directions

1. Give each student a sheet of red construction paper.
2. Hand out the rest of the materials.
3. Help students with tracing, cutting, gluing, and writing.

Student Directions

1. Trace your hand onto red construction paper and cut out.
2. Write your name on the hand using a marker.
3. Glue your red hand to any of the appropriate seven stripes on the flag mural, as shown by your teacher.
4. Think what "Hands Across America" or the flag means to you, and write a few words to explain it in any of the white stripes.

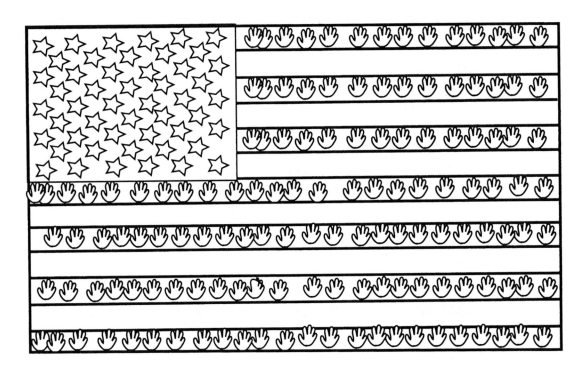

162

58. FLAG MOBILE

Grade Level: 1–5

The U.S. flag is made up of fifty stars (one for each state) on a field of blue and thirteen red and white stripes (one stripe for each of the original colonies). The red signifies courage; the white, liberty; and the blue, loyalty.

Project Description

Students will create a flag mobile.

Advance Preparation

Make one copy of the stars pattern sheet for each student. Cut seven 1-3/8" x 12" red paper strips for each student. Cut two 24" lengths of string for each student. Cut three 2" x 12" strips of crepe paper of each color (red, white, and blue) for each student. Have enough sheets of 12" x 18" white and red construction paper to give one to each student.

Materials Needed

Stars pattern sheets
12" x 18" sheets of white construction paper
12" x 18" sheets of red construction paper
String
Red, white, and blue crepe paper
Scissors
Blue markers
Glue
Stapler
Hole punch

Connections to Other Disciplines

Social Studies: Discuss the history of the American flag and its many designs.

Cooking: Have fun with different foods. Can students think of foods that are red (such as strawberries, apples, tomatoes), white (such as rice,

bread, milk), and blue (blueberries)? Let students experience samples of these various foods.

Reading: Introduce *Red, White, and Blue: The Story of the American Flag* by John Herman.

Teacher Directions

1. Talk about the meaning of the designs and colors on the U.S. flag.
2. Give each student one copy of the stars pattern sheet; seven red paper strips; three each of the red, white, and blue crepe paper strips; and two pieces of string.
3. Distribute the rest of the materials.
4. Help students as needed.

Student Directions

1. Use a blue marker to color the background of the stars pattern.
2. Position the seven red strips across the white paper and glue in place (see the illustration). Let dry.

18"

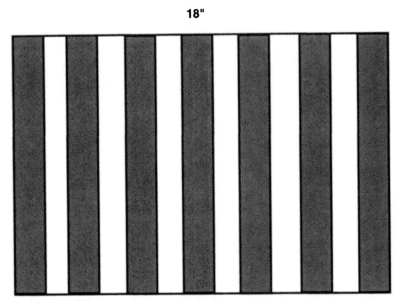

12"

3. Cut along the box of the stars pattern and glue onto the top right corner of the red and white striped paper (see the illustration).
4. Roll the paper into a cylinder using the 18" side and staple the edges together.
5. Punch four holes at equal distances around the top of the flag mobile.

164

Hands-On Art Activities

18"

12"

6. Thread two strings across the top of the flag and tie together.

7. Staple the strips of crepe paper to the bottom of the flag, alternating colors.

8. Hang the flag mobiles in the classroom.

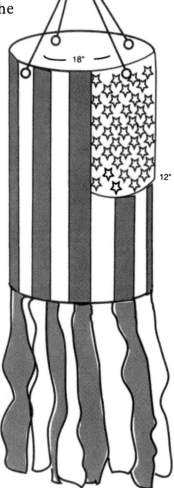

18"

12"

Father's Day

59. SHIRT AND TIE

Grade Level: K–2

Father's Day celebrates all of the wonderful contributions fathers make to their families every day. Even if your father doesn't wear a tie, he'll appreciate this handmade card. (*Note:* Be sensitive to individual student's family situations.)

Project Description

Students will create a shirt and tie card for Father's Day.

Advance Preparation

Make one copy of the tie and shirt pocket pattern sheet for each student.

Materials Needed

   Tie and shirt pocket pattern sheets

   11" x 14" sheets of colored construction paper

   Markers

   Glue

   Scissors

   Rulers

Connections to Other Disciplines

Social Studies: Why is George Washington called "the father of our country"?

Science: Talk about animal fathers, and how some animal fathers, such as the emperor penguin, help raise the babies.

Reading: Introduce *Papa, Please Get the Moon for Me* by Eric Carle.

Teacher Directions

1. Give each student a tie and shirt pocket pattern sheet.
2. Hand out the rest of the materials.
3. Help students with cutting and folding.

Student Directions

1. Draw a horizontal line 2" from the top of the paper.
2. Cut 3" on both sides on the line.
3. To form the shirt's collar, fold down the two top corners to meet at the line.
4. Color the tie and shirt pocket and cut them out.
5. Glue the tie and pocket to the shirt.
6. Draw a handkerchief coming out of the pocket and either color it or write a Father's Day message on it.

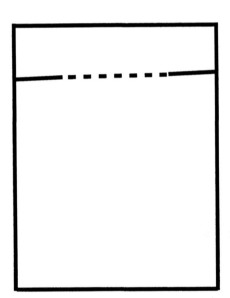
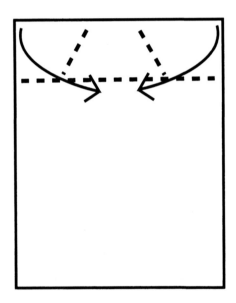

I ♥ You Dad

60. BEAR CANDY BOX

Grade Level: 2–3
Give Dad some candies for Father's Day in this handmade gift!

Project Description
Students will create a three-dimensional box. (*Note:* Be sensitive to individual student's family situations.)

Advance Preparation
Make one copy of the bear box pattern sheet for each student. Bring in wrapped candies to put in the finished boxes.

Materials Needed
Bear box pattern sheets   Tape

Markers or crayons   Wrapped candies

Scissors

Connections to Other Disciplines
Mathematics: Discuss shapes (rectangle, cube) and how to calculate the volume of a box.

Teacher Directions
1. Give each student a copy of the bear box pattern sheet.
2. Distribute the rest of the materials.
3. Help students with cutting, folding, and taping.

Student Directions
1. Cut out the bear box pattern.
2. Color the pattern on the front and back.
3. Cut along the bold lines.
4. Fold on the dotted lines to form a box. (You may fold the box so that the bear's face is on either the inside or the outside of the box.)
5. Tape the sides of the box together.
6. Fill the box with wrapped candies.

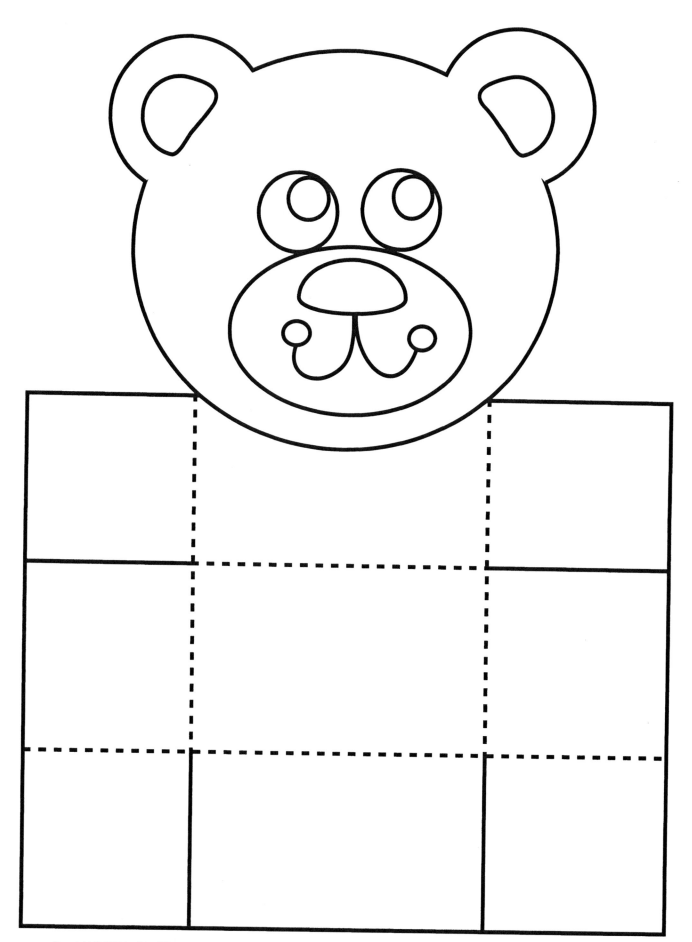

Design Activities

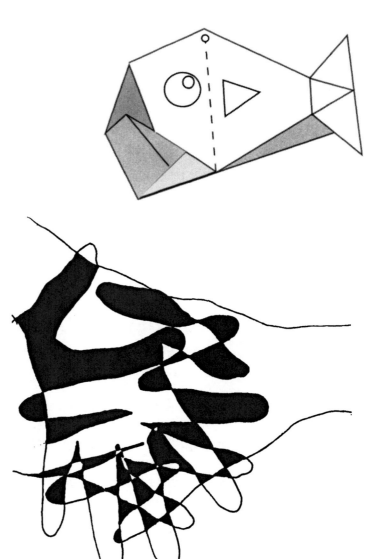

Weaving

61. MAGAZINE PAPER WEAVING

Grade Level: 3–5

Weaving is an ancient art that can be done with many different materials. This project uses paper weaving to teach the basic over-and-under technique.

Project Description

Students will create a paper weaving using magazine pictures.

Advance Preparation

Collect full-page magazine pictures that have bright colors, simple shapes, and interesting designs. You might check out fashion figures, gardening, and home design magazines. Use one 12" x 18" sheet of construction paper for storing work in progress.

Materials Needed

Magazines

Scissors

Tape

Rulers

12" x 18" sheets of white construction paper for backing

Pencils or markers

One 12" x 18" sheet of construction paper to fold and store magazine strips for each student

Connections to Other Disciplines

Social Studies: Discuss the history of weaving and its importance to different cultures, such as those of Native Americans.

Mathematics: Talk about and display geometric designs found in weavings.

Reading: Introduce *Songs from the Loom: A Navajo Girl Learns to Weave* by Monty Roessel and *Weaving a California Tradition: A Native American Basketmaker* by Linda Yumane.

Teacher Directions

1. Have students each choose two magazine pictures.
2. Show students the weaving technique of "over and under."
3. Help students as needed.

Student Directions

1. Choose two magazine pictures with shapes and colors that work together; for example, two faces, two colorful architectural designs, two figures.

2. Using a ruler and pencil, mark off vertical lines, 1" apart, across one picture (see illustration). *Important:* Leave a 1/2" horizontal holding strip at the top of the picture.

3. On the other picture, draw horizontal lines one inch apart; do *not* leave a top holding strip. These strips will form the weft that is woven over and under the strips of the first picture. Mark the strips lightly with small numbers (1, 2, 3, etc.) in case the strips get out of order when you weave.

4. Cut out the horizontal strips of the second picture.

5. Take each horizontal strip in order of its position, top to bottom, and interweave it with the vertical strips of the first picture.

6. When the two pictures are interwoven, tape the edges on the back and tape the completed weaving to a construction paper backing.

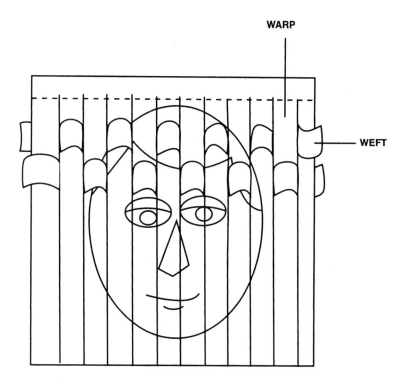

WARP

WEFT

Design Activities   **175**

Crafts

62. CRAFT STICK NECKLACE

Grade Level: 3–5

People have made and used flags for over four thousand years. The first flags were made of wood or metal. Later, flags were constructed of fabric. Flags are used as messages and as symbols of groups and countries. Today every country of the world has a flag that symbolizes its citizens' pride.

Project Description

Students will use craft sticks to create a flag necklace.

Advance Preparation

Obtain samples of flags from around the world to display in the classroom. Get a supply of craft sticks (ten to twelve per student), yarn, oak tag, and white tempera paint. Cut yarn into 18" lengths (one for each student).

Materials Needed

Craft sticks
Newsprint and pencils for sketching ideas
Yarn
Colored markers
Oak tag
Scissors
White tempera paint
Paintbrushes
Tape
Glue
Newspaper to cover work area

Connections to Other Disciplines

Social Studies: Ask students to select a country and write a report about that country's flag, including the flag's history and meaning of its design.

Reading: Introduce *Flag Lore of All Nations* by Whitney Smith.

176

Teacher Directions

1. Display the various world flags.
2. Cover the work area with newspaper.
3. Give each student ten to twelve craft sticks and a sheet of oak tag.
4. Hand out the rest of the materials.
5. Help students with assembling, as needed.

Student Directions

1. First think of an original design for a flag. You might want to show something about your heritage, your family, or your town.
2. Make a rough drawing of your flag on newsprint so that you can plan your design.
3. When you're ready to start making the necklace, line up your craft sticks on your sheet of oak tag.
4. Trace around the sticks and then cut the oak tag to that size.
5. Now glue the sticks onto this cut sheet of oak tag. Let dry.
6. Paint all of the sticks with white tempera paint. Let dry.
7. Using your rough drawing as a guide, use markers to create your flag design on the craft sticks. Remember to color the edges of the sticks, too.

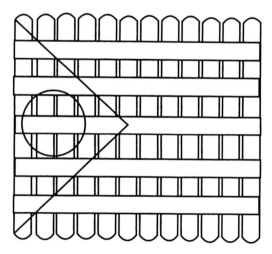

8. When finished, attach the yarn to the back of the necklace with tape. Wear your flag necklace with pride!

 **178** **Hands-On Art Activities**

63. BINGO-STYLE GAME

Grade Level: 1–3

Children of all ages enjoy bingo. It's even more fun when you make your own game board.

Project Description

Students will create a bingo-style game.

Advance Preparation

Obtain poker chips or other tokens as game pieces. Purchase small prizes for winners. Make one copy of the bingo pattern sheet for each student.

Materials Needed

8-1/2" x 11" sheets of construction paper

Crayons

Poker chips or other tokens

Small prizes

Bingo pattern sheets

Scissors

Glue

Bowl

Connections to Other Disciplines

Mathematics: Discuss directionality (vertical, horizontal, diagonal) and columns and rows.

Music: Sing the song "B-I-N-G-O."

Language Arts: Have students select three or four pictures from the game board and write a story that uses those items.

Teacher Directions

1. Give each student one copy of the bingo pattern sheet.
2. Distribute the rest of the materials, except for the bowl and small prizes.
3. Make a copy of the pattern for yourself, cut it apart into the sixteen boxes, fold each one in half, and place them in a bowl.

Design Activities   **179**

4. Help students with their boards, as needed.

5. When everyone's board is done, go over the rules for playing bingo. Most students will already know how to play the game, but talk about the game to refresh everyone's memory.

6. Play the game by pulling the pieces out of the bowl one at a time and calling out the name of the object until someone gets bingo! Give that person a prize and play again.

Student Directions

1. Color each picture on the bingo pattern sheet.

2. Cut the boxes apart. Set aside.

3. Fold the construction paper in half, then in half again, then in half again, and then in half again.

4. Open up the paper: the folds have marked sixteen boxes.

5. Take a picture box and glue it in any one of the boxes on your construction paper. Do the same with the other fifteen pictures.

6. Your bingo board is finished. Now use the poker chips to cover the pictures your teacher calls out. Let's play bingo!

SUN	FISH	TREE	NAME
TRIANGLE	BUG	CAT	BOAT
BUTTERFLY	HOUSE	RABBIT	FLOWER
CUP	HEART	BASEBALL	STAR

64. PAPIER-MÂCHÉ BOWL

Grade Level: 3–5

Papier-mâché means "chewed paper" in French. This technique of making objects out of mashed up paper and some kind of glue actually originated in China about two thousand years ago, but it didn't become popular in Europe until the eighteenth century. This project is a bit more complicated than most of the others in this book, but the results are well worth it.

Project Description

Students will create a durable bowl using papier-mâché and paints. (*Note:* This project will be done in four lessons.)

Advance Preparation

Obtain a 6" paper bowl for each student. Obtain examples of pottery and bowls from different cultures. Just prior to beginning the activity, mix equal parts Elmer's Glue-All and water in small paper cups.

Materials Needed

6" paper bowls
Newsprint (or lightweight copier paper)
Small paper cups
Elmer's Glue-All
Water
Paintbrushes
Drawing paper
Colored pencils
Markers
Newspaper to cover work area
Acrylic gloss

Connections to Other Disciplines

Social Studies: Discuss how bowls (and pottery) have been used by various cultures, such as the Aztec, African, Native American, Inuit, and Asian peoples.

Mathematics: Study patterns and geometric designs.

Language Arts: Have students write stories or role-play about how bowls were used by different cultures. Were they used at mealtime? As art for display? Sold to earn money?

Reading: Introduce *Children of Clay: A Family of Potters* by Rina Swentzell.

Teacher Directions

Lesson 1
Distribute the bowls, newsprint, cups of glue and water mixture, and paintbrushes.

Lesson 2
1. Display samples of pottery and bowls from other cultures.
2. Distribute colored pencils and drawing paper.

Lesson 3
1. Distribute markers.
2. Help students as needed.

Lesson 4
1. Distribute acrylic gloss and paintbrushes.
2. Help students as needed.

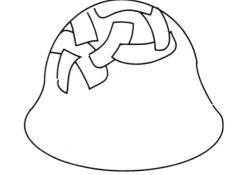

Student Directions

Lesson 1
1. Tear the newsprint into small pieces and glue them to the inside and outside of the paper bowl. Let dry.
2. Use a paintbrush and the glue and water mixture to cover the pieces of paper inside and outside of the bowl. Let dry.

Glue + Water

Lesson 2

Use the drawing paper and colored pencils to create a rough sketch of the design you want to use on the bowl. To help you get started, look at the sample designs provided.

Lesson 3

Copy your design onto the bowl using markers. Be sure to add as much graphic detail as possible.

Lesson 4

1. Use a paintbrush to apply a coat of acrylic gloss to the inside and outside of your bowl. Let dry.
2. Apply a second coat of acrylic gloss. Let dry.

65. TRIANGLE SCULPTURE

Grade Level: 3–5

Sculptures can be created with anything from marble to found objects. Whatever the artist can imagine can become a sculpture!

Project Description

Students will create a three-dimensional sculpture made of coffee stirrers and colored tissue paper.

Advance Preparation

Obtain 2" x 8" blocks of wood, one for each student. Buy coffee stirrers and tissue paper in different colors. Have a glue gun handy (CAUTION: for adult use only).

Materials Needed

Coffee stirrers

Glue

Tissue paper in different colors

Scissors

Markers

2" x 8" blocks of wood for bases of finished sculptures

Glue gun (CAUTION: for adult use only)

Connections to Other Disciplines

Social Studies: Explore the uses of triangles in architecture. Discuss the pyramids in Egypt and the entrance to the Louvre in Paris, France.

Mathematics: Discuss the different kinds of triangles (right, acute, obtuse).

Reading: Introduce *The Greedy Triangle* by Marilyn Burns and *Building Toothpick Bridges* by Jeanne Pollard.

Teacher Directions

1. Distribute the materials.
2. Help students as needed.
3. Use the glue gun to attach the sculptures to the bases.

Student Directions

1. Glue together coffee stirrers to make eight to ten triangles. Let dry.
2. Trace each coffee stirrer triangle onto different colors of tissue paper.
3. Cut out the tissue paper triangles and glue them to the coffee stirrer triangles. Let each triangle shape dry before assembling.
4. Assemble the triangles into a three-dimensional sculpture by overlapping and gluing the pieces in place. Add extra glue as needed for support. Let dry.
5. Use markers to decorate the wooden base.

Your teacher will use the glue gun to attach your sculpture to the base.

Mobiles

66. SEA LIFE MOBILE

Grade Level: 1–4

The oceans are brimming with a variety of sea life. Here's a way to celebrate life under the sea with art.

Project Description

Students will create an ocean scene using cut paper and paper plates.

Advance Preparation

Obtain pictures of underwater life (fish, coral, sea horses, and so on). Purchase large white paper plates, one for each student. Have white paper, various colors of construction paper, and string.

Materials Needed

Underwater life pictures

Large white paper plates

White paper, one sheet, for punched dots

Construction paper in various colors

Hole punch

String

Markers or crayons

Scissors

Glue

Connections to Other Disciplines

Science: Discuss the different kinds of sea life and plants that live in oceans and rivers. Talk about saltwater and freshwater fish. What happens when pollutants enter the water system?

Language Arts: Have students write a story about living under water. Where would they live? What would they eat? What would they wear? How would they travel?

Reading: Introduce *Fish Is Fish* by Leo Lionni, *Here Is the Coral Reef* by Madeleine Dunphy, *The Magic School Bus on the Ocean Floor* by Joanna Cole, *What Makes an Ocean Wave? Questions and Answers About Oceans and Ocean Life* by Melvin Berger and Gilda Berger, and *The Deep Sea* by Bruce H. Robison.

Teacher Directions

1. Display the pictures you've collected of underwater life and describe some of the creatures.
2. Distribute the rest of the materials.
3. Help students with cutting and gluing.

Student Directions

1. Color the paper plate as the ocean floor and water.
2. On the construction paper, use markers or crayons to draw different fish, seashells, other sea life, and plants that live underwater.
3. Cut out your pictures.
4. Glue each picture onto your ocean scene. Layer the pictures.
5. Punch holes from the white paper.
6. Glue these white circles onto the plate to represent air bubbles.
7. Punch a hole at the top of the ocean plate, insert a string, and hang the ocean scene with your classmates' scenes to make a large sea life mobile.

67. ORIGAMI FISH MOBILE

Grade Level: 3–5

Origami is an ancient Japanese art of folding squares of paper into representational shapes.

Project Description

Students will create an origami fish mobile.

Advance Preparation

Make three copies of the fish pattern for each student. Obtain 1' sticks (one for each student) to suspend the origami fish. Bring in finished examples of origami to show students.

Materials Needed

Origami examples

Fish pattern sheets

Crayons

Scissors

String

1' sticks

Hole punch

Glue

Connections to Other Disciplines

Science: What different kinds of fish might be found in the waters around Japan?

Cooking: Talk about sushi (cold rice formed into various shapes and garnished with pieces of raw fish or shellfish).

Reading: Introduce *The Fish from Japan* by Elizabeth K. Cooper and *Building with Paper* by E. Richard Churchill.

Teacher Directions

1. Show students the samples of origami you have collected. Tell students they will be making a modified origami.
2. Give each student three copies of the fish pattern sheet and a stick.
3. Distribute the rest of the materials.
4. Explain how to fold the fish.
5. Help students as needed.

Student Directions

1. Color and make designs on each of the three fish patterns.
2. Cut out the three fish.
3. Fold inward along all of the dotted lines, then glue each adjacent flap, connecting the sides of the fish into a three-dimensional shape. Connect A to B, C to D, E to F, and G to H (see illustration).
4. Punch a hole at the top of each fish.
5. Tie a different length of string to each fish. Then tie each string to your stick.
6. Hang your origami fish mobile.

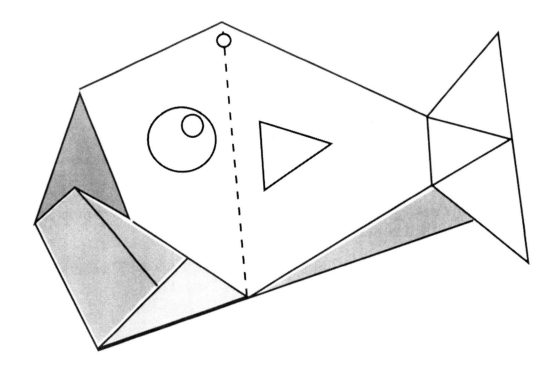

Hands-On Art Activities

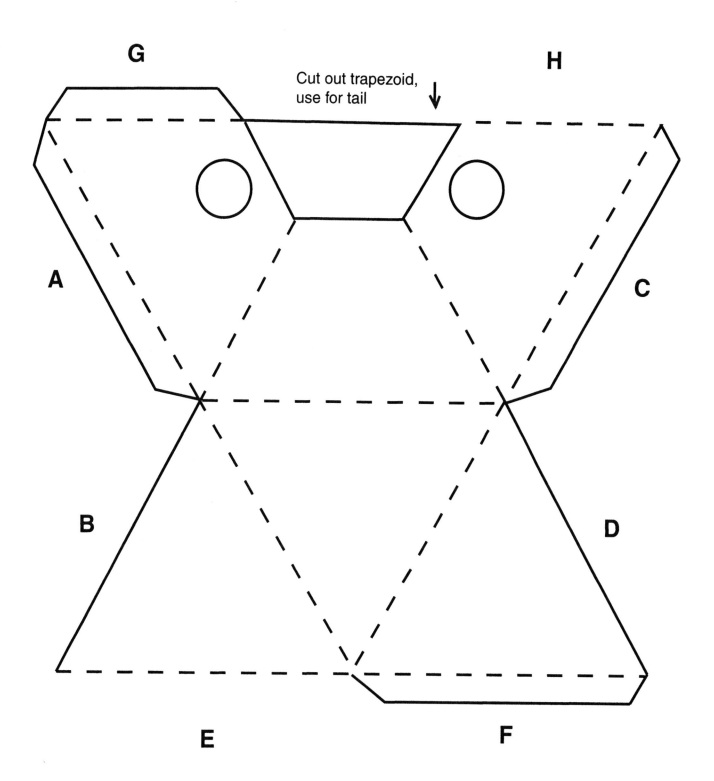

G H

Cut out trapezoid,
use for tail ↓

A C

B D

E F

Frames

68. ANIMAL COOKIE PICTURE FRAME

Grade Level: 1–3

This project shows how to use unusual items to create wonderful art. Kids love doing this project, plus they get to snack on the extra animal cookies!

Project Description

Students will create frames using animal cookies to make designs.

Advance Preparation

Buy animal cookies (at least six per student, plus extras for snacking) and one paper plate for each student. Obtain enough corrugated cardboard boxes to make a frame for each student. Each frame should be 6" x 8" with a 3" x 4" opening.

Materials Needed

Corrugated cardboard

Animal cookies

Paints

Paintbrushes

Newspaper to cover work area

Glue

Paper plates

Crayons

Connections to Other Disciplines

Social Studies: Talk about families and how many families display photographs of family members around their homes. Do any of the students have photos of their grandparents, great-grandparents, and other older family members when these people were much younger? How did their clothing look many, many years ago? What about hair styles?

Reading: Introduce *Family Pictures* by Carmen Lomas Garza.

Teacher Directions

1. Give each student a corrugated cardboard picture frame and a paper plate.
2. Distribute the rest of the materials.
3. Let students snack on the animal cookies, but make sure they don't eat any painted ones.
4. Help students as needed.

Student Directions

1. Write your name in crayon on the back of the frame and on the back of the paper plate.
2. Paint your frame in whatever color you would like. Set aside to dry.
3. Take six animal cookies and paint each one in whatever colors you would like. (You can eat a few *unpainted* cookies if you like.)
4. Place the painted cookies on your paper plate. Let dry.
5. Glue the painted animal cookies onto your frame.
6. Bring your photo frame home and use it to display a picture of yourself or a member of your family.

Pop-Ups

69. LEAPING DOLPHIN

Grade Level: 3–4
Kinetic art is art in motion, like the moving dolphin in this fun project.

Project Description
Students will create a three-dimensional moving sculpture of a dolphin out of oak tag and pipe cleaners.

Advance Preparation
Obtain pictures of dolphins. Make a copy of the dolphin and waves pattern sheets for each student. Buy pipe cleaners and cut them into 4" lengths (one for each student).

Materials Needed
Dolphin and waves pattern sheets

9" x 12" sheets of white oak tag

Markers or crayons

Pipe cleaners

Scissors

Transparent tape

Connections to Other Disciplines
Science: Discuss the differences between a dolphin and a porpoise. Talk about the importance of conserving all sea life.

Language Arts: Have students pretend they are oceanographers (people who study the oceans and sea life), and ask them to write about or role-play a day in their life as an oceanographer. What are they wearing? Where do they work? What are they presently investigating?

Reading: Introduce *Is a Dolphin a Fish? Questions and Answers About Dolphins* by Melvin and Gilda Berger.

194

Teacher Directions

1. Display the pictures of dolphins.
2. Give each student a copy of the pattern sheet, a sheet of oak tag, and a pipe cleaner.
3. Distribute the rest of the materials.
4. Help students as needed.

Student Directions

1. Cut out the dolphin, waves, and stand patterns.
2. Trace the patterns on the oak tag.
3. Cut out the traced oak tag patterns.
4. Color both sides of the dolphin, the waves, and the stand.
5. Cut the slits on the waves and stand (as shown on patterns) and fit together.
6. Tape one end of the pipe cleaner to the dolphin.
7. Tape the other end of the pipe cleaner to an ocean wave.
8. Watch your dolphin jump out of the ocean!

70. CITYSCAPE

Grade Level: 3–5

In this project, students will learn how to work with foreground and background as they create a city scene.

Project Description

Students will create a three-dimensional cityscape using cereal boxes, cut paper, and toys.

Advance Preparation

Collect empty individual-sized cereal boxes and other small boxes (at least two for each student). Obtain or have students bring in small toys of people, cars, trucks, dogs, and cats. Or just draw cars, pets, and people on white paper with a small flap on the bottom of each. Cut and fold flaps to stand the shapes in front of the buildings and other elements of a city scene.

Materials Needed

9" x 12" sheets of white drawing paper

Small individual cereal or similar sized boxes

Colored construction paper

Glue

Scissors

Markers or crayons

Small toys of people, trees, cars, and so on

Connections to Other Disciplines

Social Studies: Discuss the city, town, or rural area in which the students live. Do students know the history of their town? Who were the first settlers?

Mathematics: Explore grids. Explain that the streets of many cities (such as New York City) are designed as grids, with streets forming parallel and perpendicular lines.

Reading: Introduce *Garden in the City* by Gerda Muller and *Greening the City Streets* by Barbara A. Huff.

Teacher Directions

1. Give each student two small boxes and the other materials. Keep the small toys in a central location.
2. Help students with assembly, as needed.

Student Directions

1. Fold the white paper in half and open halfway.
2. Glue the two small boxes to the paper as shown. These will be the bases for your city buildings.
3. Draw two buildings on construction paper and cut them out.
4. Decorate the buildings with markers or crayons in whatever way you like.
5. Glue your cutout buildings to the two small boxes.
6. Use some of the small toys of cars, trees, pets, trucks, plants, and so on, to complete your cityscape.
7. What will you name your city?

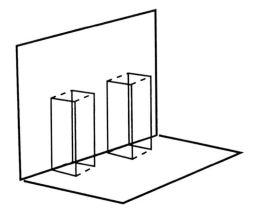

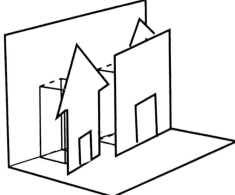

Puppets

71. FLOWER FINGER PUPPET

Grade Level: K–2

Puppets date back thousands of years. Shadow and rod puppets and marionettes have been popular in the Far East, and many of them are quite beautiful works of art. Today puppets can be found in art museums as well as on TV and even in Broadway shows!

Project Description

Students will create a flower finger puppet using felt, wiggly eyes, and pom-poms.

Advance Preparation

Create a base for the puppet for each student by rolling a 4" x 4" piece of colored paper into a cylinder and taping the seam. Obtain two sets of wiggly eyes and a yellow pom-pom for each student. Make a copy of the flower pattern sheet for each student. Buy three different colors of felt and cut two 3" square pieces of felt and one 2" square piece of felt (one in each color) for each student.

Materials Needed

    Colored paper

    Colored felt

    Flower pattern sheets

    Scissors

    Wiggly eyes

    1/2" yellow pom-poms

    Glue

    Black markers

Connections to Other Disciplines

Science: Discuss the relationship between flowers and insects. Why do bees fly from flower to flower?

Language Arts: Have students use their finger puppets to create stories of what flowers and bees might say to each other.

Reading: Introduce *Bees, Wasps, and Ants* by George S. Fichter, *Fran's Flower* by Lisa Bruce, and *Garden* by Robert Maass.

Teacher Directions

1. Give each student a colored paper cylinder to use as a base for the puppet.
2. Give each student a copy of the flower pattern sheet, two 3" square pieces of felt, one 2" square piece of felt, two pairs of wiggly eyes, and a yellow pom-pom.
3. Distribute the rest of the materials.
4. Help students with gluing and assembling.

Student Directions

1. Cut out the three flower parts from the pattern sheet. Trace around each piece on a different color of felt. (Use the two larger pieces of felt for the two flowers and the smaller piece of felt for the circle.)
2. Glue the smaller flower on top of the larger flower.
3. Glue the circle on top of the flower.
4. Glue two wiggly eyes to the circle.
5. Draw a smile on the circle.
6. Glue the yellow pom-pom to the flower to make a bee.
7. Glue two wiggly eyes to the bee.
8. Glue the flower to the base. Your finger puppet is finished!

Paper Folding

72. ACCORDION-PLAYING BEAR

Grade Level: K–3

The accordion, an instrument popular in German, Swiss, and Polish music, dates back to 1831. Knowing how to make an accordion shape out of paper, as students learn in this project, is a useful art skill.

Project Description

Students will make a paper bear holding an accordion.

Advance Preparation

Make one copy of the bear pattern and one copy of the accordion pattern for each student. If possible, bring in an actual accordion, or bring in pictures of accordions.

Materials Needed

Bear pattern sheets
Accordion pattern sheets
Scissors
Crayons
Glue

Connections to Other Disciplines

Social Studies: Discuss various instruments and how each can be associated with different cultures. For example, the accordion is popular in German, Swiss, and Polish music; the flute is important to Irish and Scottish music; drums are associated with African, Native American, and Hispanic music; and so on.

Music: Bring in actual instruments, or listen to recordings that illustrate various instruments. Try to find *The Carnival of Animals* by Saint-Saëns or *The Young Person's Guide to the Orchestra* by Britten.

Reading: Introduce *Crash! Bang! Boom!* by Peter Spier, *Making Musical Things* by Ann Wiseman, and "Musical Instruments of the World" series by Barrie Carson Turner.

Teacher Directions

1. Display the real accordion (or show pictures).
2. Give each student a bear pattern sheet and an accordion pattern sheet.
3. Distribute the rest of the materials.
4. Help students with cutting, folding, and gluing.

Student Directions

1. Draw a face on and color the bear.
2. Cut out the bear.
3. Fold the accordion cutout back and forth on the dotted lines, as seen in the diagram. Your teacher can help you, if needed.
4. Glue one end of the accordion to one of the bear's paws.
5. Glue the other end of the accordion to the bear's other paw.

What song do you think the bear is playing?

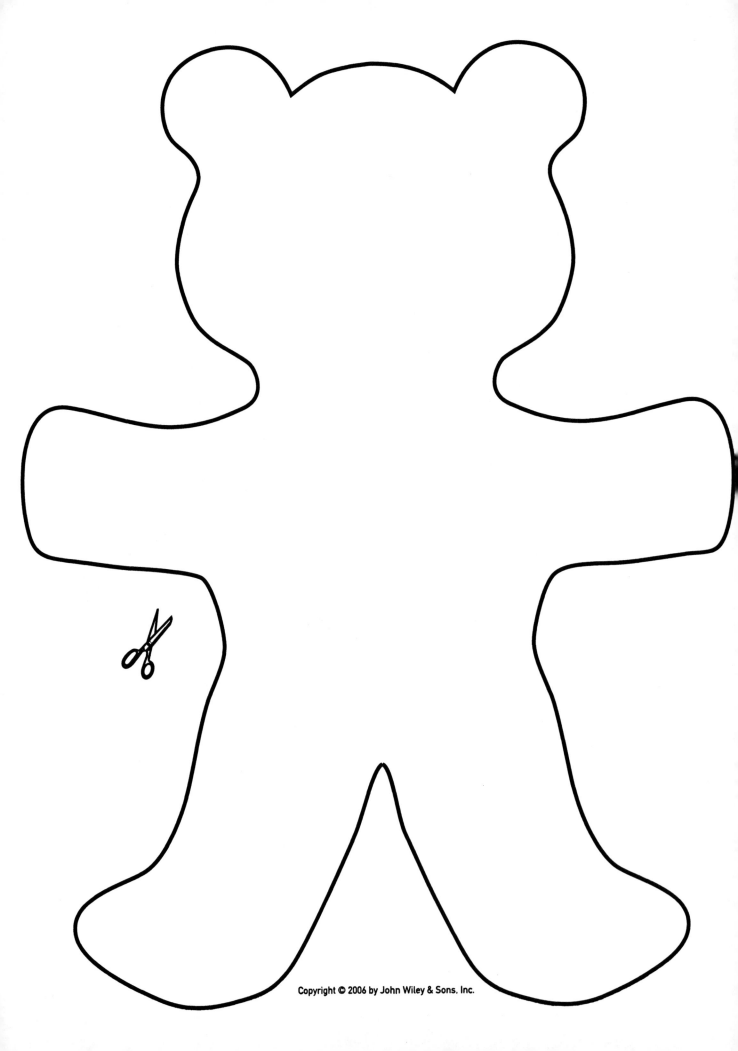

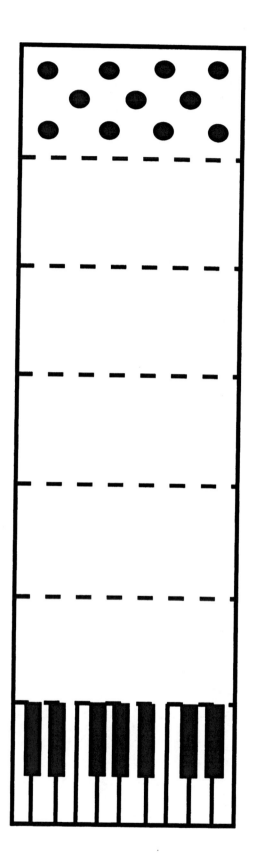

Drawing

73. JIGSAW PUZZLE

Grade Level: K–2

Jigsaw puzzles are a fun way to help students develop thinking skills and part-to-whole coordination.

Project Description

Students will make a drawing using a pattern of repeating shapes. Then they will make their drawing into a jigsaw puzzle.

Advance Preparation

Cut white drawing paper into 8" squares, one for each student. Obtain zip-locking plastic bags.

Materials Needed

White drawing paper

Scissors

Glue

Crayons

Zip-locking plastic bags

Connections to Other Disciplines

Math: Discuss patterns and shapes.

Reading: Introduce *ABCDiscovery! An Alphabet Book of Picture Puzzles* by Izhar Cohen and *Anno's Magic Seeds* by Anno Mitsumasa.

Teacher Directions

1. Give each student one 8" square of white paper and one plastic bag.
2. Distribute the rest of the materials.
3. Help students as needed.

Student Directions

1. Think of a simple shape, such as a fish, heart, or flower.
2. Draw the shape in different sizes all over your drawing paper to make an interesting pattern.
3. Color the shapes.
4. Fold your paper in half, then in half again, then in half again, and then in half again.
5. Open the paper; the folds mark sixteen squares.
6. Turn over the paper and number the back of each square, 1 through 16.
7. Cut out the sixteen squares and put them into a plastic bag. Seal it and shake the bag to mix up the squares.
8. Now take out the sixteen squares and try to assemble your puzzle (without looking at the numbers!).

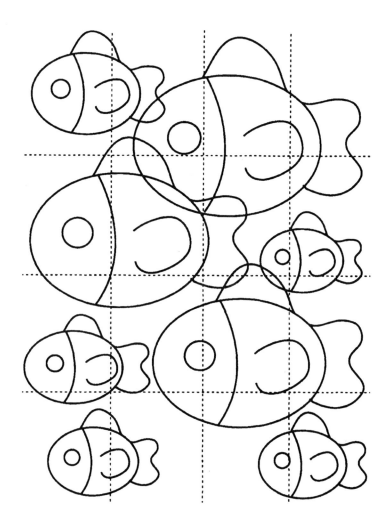

74. ARC PATTERNS

Grade Level: K–5

In this project, students will use overlapping concentric arcs to make interesting patterns. When colored, the results can look like stained glass.

Project Description

Students will create overlapping concentric arc designs using paper plates.

Advance Preparation

Buy paper plates (any size). Make finished examples of some arc designs. Cut one 6" square of white drawing paper for each student. Bring a color wheel to the class.

Materials Needed

Paper plates

White drawing paper

Scissors

Crayons, markers, craypas, or colored pencils

Color wheel

Connections to Other Disciplines

Science: Talk about the color spectrum.

Mathematics: Discuss concentric circles and arcs.

Reading: Introduce *Circles: Fun Ideas for Getting A-round in Math* by Catherine Ross and *The Magic Wand and Other Bright Experiments on Light and Color* by Paul Doherty.

Teacher Directions

1. Display your finished samples of arc designs.
2. Give each student a paper plate and a 6" square of white drawing paper.
3. Distribute the rest of the materials.

4. When they are ready to color, show students the color wheel and talk about different types of color combinations (monochromatic colors are one color plus a tint or shade; analogous colors, such as blue and purple, are adjacent on the color wheel; and complementary colors, such as green and red, are opposite on the color wheel).

Student Directions

1. Fold the paper plate in half and cut out the inner circle, leaving the rim of the outer circle intact. Set aside the inner circle.
2. Use the inner and outer parts of the rim to draw concentric arcs on the drawing paper. Be sure to overlap them.
3. Choose color combinations for filling in each section of the arcs.
4. Color your picture.

75. CREATE-A-PERSON BOOK

Grade Level: 1–3
Here's a fun book that students can put together and use to make people with mixed-up parts!

Project Description
Students will draw different body parts and create a book with interchangeable sections.

Advance Preparation
Make three copies of the book page pattern sheet for each student. Have one sheet of 9" x 12" oak tag for each student.

Materials Needed
Book page pattern sheets
9" x 12" sheets of oak tag
Stapler
Pencils, crayons, or markers
Scissors

Connections to Other Disciplines
Science: Discuss different parts of the body.

Language Arts: Have students use their books to create stories about the people formed.

Reading: Introduce *The Amazing Pull-Out Pop-Up Body in a Book* by David Hawcock, *How Do I Know It's Yucky? And Other Questions About the Senses* by Sharon Cromwell, and *Whoever You Are* by Mem Fox.

Teacher Directions
1. On the chalkboard, draw a sample page for a create-a-person book and explain the different sections and what they could look like. For example:
   - The HAT/HAIR section (top hat? baseball cap? curly hair?)
   - The HEAD section (a happy face? a sad face? a freckled face?)

- The BODY + ARMS section (a jacket? a raincoat? gloves?)
- The LEGS + FEET section (a skirt? pants? shorts? sandals?)

2. Give each student three copies of the book page pattern sheet.
3. Distribute the rest of the materials, except for the oak tag.
4. Help students as needed.
5. Collect the students' finished pages and insert each student's pages into a folded sheet of oak tag. Staple the cover and pages together on the outside fold.

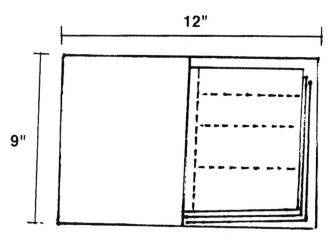

6. Return the covered pages to each student and let the students decorate their covers.
7. Help students cut apart the sections.

Student Directions

1. Think of three different people you would like to draw.
2. On each page, draw a different person. Remember to keep the different body parts in each section.
3. Color your drawings.
4. Give your drawings to your teacher, who will put a cover on your book.
5. When your teacher returns the book to you, color and decorate the front cover.

6. Open the book and cut along the three lines on each page to separate the sections.
7. Now flip back the different sections to create different people!

Design Activities

5 1/2"

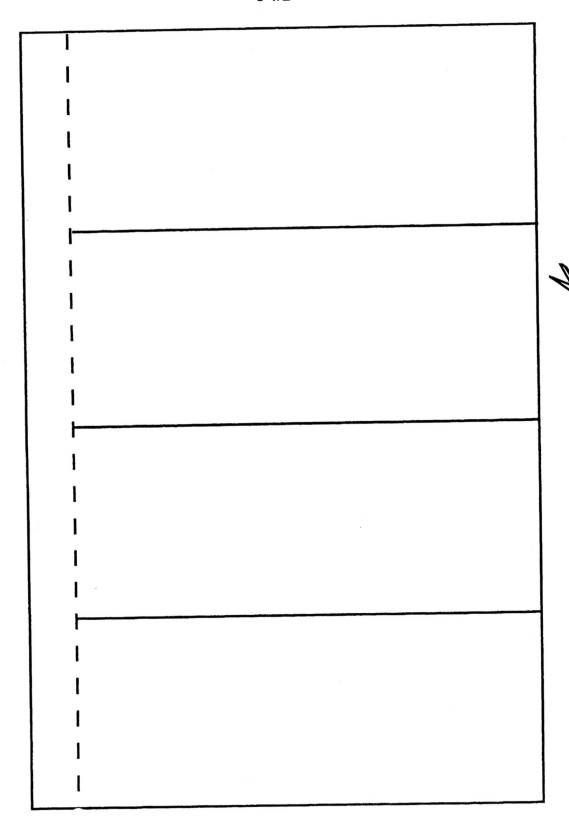

8"

76. OVERLAPPING HANDS

Grade Level: 1–4

This project is a study in positive and negative space using overlapping hands. Students will learn about foreground and background perspectives as they create interesting patterns.

Project Description

Students will create a design of positive and negative space.

Advance Preparation

Obtain samples of art or designs that use positive and negative space, such as checkerboard patterns, Native American rug patterns, Islamic patterns, and paintings by Miro and Mondrian. Have enough 12" x 18" sheets of white drawing paper to give one to each student.

Materials Needed

  12" x 18" sheets of white drawing paper

  Pencils

  Crayons or colored pencils

Connections to Other Disciplines

Mathematics: Discuss positive and negative numbers.

Science: Explore optical illusions. Check out the works by M. C. Escher.

Reading: Introduce *The King's Chessboard* by David Birch.

Teacher Directions

1. As you show the samples you collected, talk about positive and negative spaces and background and foreground.
2. Give each student a sheet of 12" x 18" white drawing paper.
3. Distribute the rest of the materials.
4. Help students with the tracing or coloring as needed.

Student Directions

1. Trace your hand on the white paper using a pencil. Close off the shape by drawing a line at the wrist.
2. Reposition your hand and make a new tracing.
3. Reposition your hand again and make a third tracing.
4. Look at your overall design and think of a checkerboard. You want to color your drawing so that light spaces border dark spaces, as in the examples your teacher has shown you.
5. Make pencil marks to show where the dark areas should be.
6. Use a dark colored crayon or colored pencil to color in each area indicated by your pencil marks.
7. Use a light colored crayon or colored pencil to color the rest of the sections.

Painting

77. PAINTED BUTTERFLY

Grade Level: K–4

Butterflies are beautiful creatures and wonderful examples of symmetry in nature. In this project, students will create butterfly paintings as they learn about symmetry in art.

Project Description

Students will create a butterfly with symmetrical paint designs.

Advance Preparation

Obtain pictures of butterflies and their wing designs. Make a copy of the butterfly pattern sheet for each student. Have an 8-1/2" x 11" sheet of white oak tag for each student.

Materials Needed

Butterfly and wing design pictures
Butterfly pattern sheets
Tempera paints
Paintbrushes
Scissors
8-1/2" x 11" sheets of white oak tag
Newspaper to cover work area

Connections to Other Disciplines

Science: Discuss butterflies and the variety of designs found on their wings. Explain how these designs are used as camouflage.

Mathematics: Discuss different types of symmetry

Reading: Introduce *Butterfly House* by Eve Bunting, *I Like Butterflies* by Gladys Conklin, *The Butterfly* by Patricia Polacco, *I Wish I Were a Butterfly* by James Howe and Ed Young, and *An Extraordinary Life: The Story of a Monarch Butterfly* by Laurence Pringle.

Teacher Directions

1. Show pictures of butterflies and their wing designs and discuss how they are symmetrical.
2. Cover the work area with newspaper.
3. Give each student a copy of the butterfly pattern sheet and an 8-1/2" x 11" sheet of oak tag.
4. Distribute the rest of the materials.
5. Help students with assembly, as needed.

Student Directions

1. Fold the white oak tag sheet in half, then open it.
2. Decorate only one half of the oak tag using tempera paints.
3. Fold the other half onto the painted side while the paint is still wet, and press on the paper.
4. Open the paper, and notice how the painted design has appeared on the other half of the paper. Let dry.

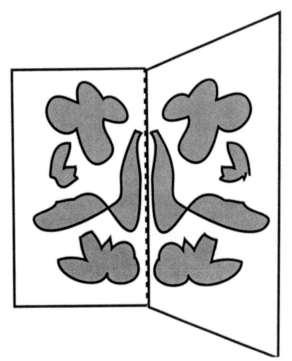

5. Fold your paper again, and trace around the half butterfly pattern on the paper at the fold.

6. Cut out the butterfly, and open up the paper. You now have a butterfly with symmetrical designs on its wings!

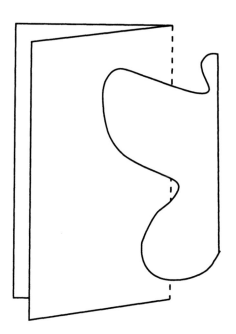

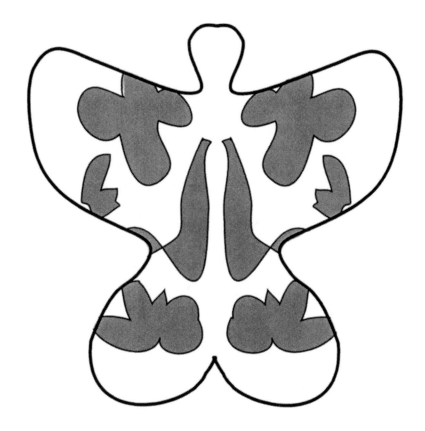

**Butterfly
Pattern**

78. DRIP PAINTING

Grade Level: 2–4
Students will use the force of gravity to help create one-of-a-kind paintings!

Project Description
Students will create a painting using dripping paint.

Advance Preparation
Be sure to have a lot of newspaper for the work area! Have enough 12" x 18" sheets of drawing paper to give one to each student.

Materials Needed
12" x 18" sheets of drawing paper
Watercolors
Paintbrushes
Water containers
Newspaper to cover work area
Black markers

Connections to Other Disciplines
Science: Discuss gravity. Can we see gravity? Can we feel gravity?

Reading: Introduce *Everything Kids Science Experiment Book: Boil Ice, Float Water, Measure Gravity—Challenge the World Around You!* by Tom Mark Robinson.

Teacher Directions
1. Show students how to do the dripping technique.
2. Distribute materials.
3. Help students as needed.

Student Directions

1. Wet the paintbrush and dip it into a watercolor.

2. Drop several drops of the watery color around the paper.

3. Pick up one edge of the paper and let the paint drip along on the paper.

4. Continue with other colors in other directions. Let dry.

5. Use a black marker to fill in some areas of the painting with lines for shading.

6. Give your drip painting a title.

Block Printing

79. LEAF PRINT COLLAGE

Grade Level: 2–5

This project uses a simple block print to create a collage.

Project Description

Students will create a leaf print collage using block prints.

Advance Preparation

Have one 5" x 7" sheet of colored tissue paper and two different colors of paint for each student. Create two leaf printing blocks for each student:

1. Cut corrugated cardboard into a 1" leaf shape.
2. Cut a 1" square of corrugated cardboard and glue it to the leaf shape (see the illustration). Let dry.

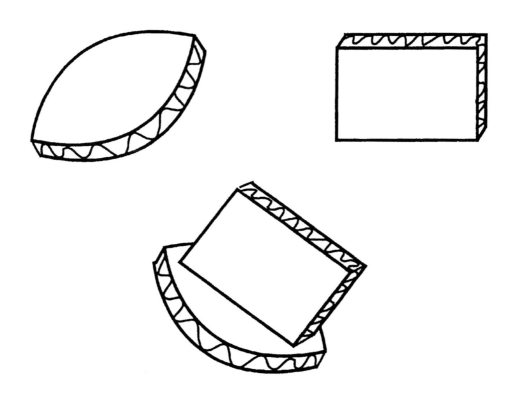

Materials Needed

5" x 7" sheets of colored tissue paper

9" x 12" sheets of white drawing paper

Leaf printing blocks (see Advance Preparation)

Paints

Scissors

Glue

Newspaper to cover work area

Connections to Other Disciplines

Science: Discuss how different colors can be made when certain colors are mixed. Talk about the color wheel and prisms.

Reading: Introduce *Autumn Leaves* by Ken Robbins.

Teacher Directions

1. Give each student two leaf printing blocks, two different colored paints, a 5" x 7" sheet of colored tissue paper, and a 9" x 12" sheet of white drawing paper.

2. Distribute the rest of the materials.

3. Help students as needed.

Student Directions

1. Fold the white drawing paper in half.

2. Cut a 4" by 3" opening along the fold (see the illustration).

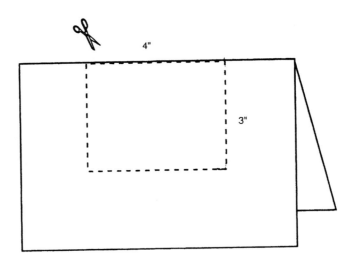

3. Open up the paper.

4. Glue the tissue paper to the back of the opening so that the tissue color fills the frame. Turn over the paper.

5. Carefully dip one of the printing blocks into paint and press the leaf print onto the border. Continue around the border and on the tissue paper.

6. Use the other printing block and paint color to make overlapping leaf prints on the tissue paper.

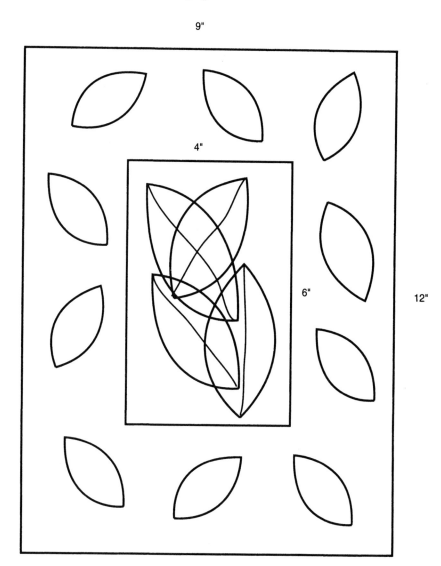

80. STRING PRINT

Grade Level: 3–5

In this block printing project, students will use string to make interesting designs and then print them on paper.

Project Description

Students will create a block print using string and cardboard.

Advance Preparation

Cut one 3" square block of corrugated cardboard and one strip of 1" x 3" corrugated cardboard for each student. Have one small dish for each student to hold paint. Have enough white drawing paper or colored construction paper to give one to each student.

Materials Needed

Corrugated cardboard

String

Glue

Pencils or markers

Tempera paints

Small dishes

White drawing paper or colored construction paper

Newspaper to cover work area

Glue gun (CAUTION: for adult use only)

Connections to Other Disciplines

Social Studies: Discuss printmaking in colonial times.

Mathematics: Explore repeating patterns and sequences.

Teacher Directions

1. Cover the work area with newspaper.
2. Give each student one 3" square block of corrugated cardboard and one 1" x 3" strip of corrugated cardboard.
3. For each student, pour about a tablespoon of tempera paint into a small dish.
4. Hand out the rest of the materials.

5. Draw some sample designs on the chalkboard.

6. Help students as needed.

Student Directions

1. Think of a simple design for your block.
2. Use pencil or marker to draw the design on the cardboard block.
3. Carefully apply glue on the design.
4. Stick the string onto the glue shape to form your design. Let dry.

 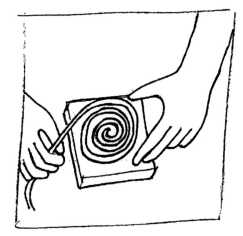

5. Your teacher will use the glue gun to adhere the cardboard strip to the back of your block. This strip is what you'll hold when making your prints.

6. Holding the cardboard strip, gently dip your block into the paint so that it covers just the string.

7. Gently press the block onto a piece of paper.

8. Repeat to make more prints on your paper. When finished, let dry.

9 780471 563396